FRONT COLOUR ILLUSTRATIONS

Front Cover: The twilight of the Met as an independent railway around 1930 at Rickmansworth. On the left, their H class 4-4-4T locomotive has just arrived with an up train and will run forward to enable a Met Bo-Bo electric to take it on to the City. Meanwhile, the regular LNER down train of empty milk tankers for Dorrington approaches behind an ex-GCR 'Director'. *(Peter Green GRA)*

Inside Cover Top: A contemporary illustration of Watkin's plans for his Wembley Park pleasure gardens and tower - inspired by his admiration for the Eiffel Tower. The actual outcome is shown on p.28. *(Brent Archive)*

Inside Cover Bottom: The scene around 1912 at the approach to Harrow where the Met and GCR tracks merge. On the left is a Met British Westinghouse 'camel-back' electric loco with Ashbury coaches and a Pullman, whilst a GCR express emerges on the right. *(F Moore/GCRS)*

Page 3 Top: A 7mm/foot scale model of Met no.27, of the classic A class 4-4-0T engines supplied by Beyer-Peacock in 1868. These sustained the needs of the Met well into the next century. *(Model & photograph Clive Foxell)*

Page 3 Bottom: In 1939, a large Robinson ex-GCR 4-6-0 express engine, now an LNER B3 no.6168 'Lord Stuart of Wortley', leaves Aylesbury with an up local. Note the vintage GCR brake-composite leading coach and the PO wagons in the sidings. *(Colour-Rail NE110/Pendragon)*

Page 4 Top: Neasden LNER shed a year after they had acquired most of the Met locomotives from LT. Ex-Met H class 4-4-4T has become a LNER class H2 no.6420, whilst behind are ex-GCR engines B7 no.5469 and class D11 no.5504, 'Jutland'. The scene is being captured by the schoolboy with a box 'Brownie'. *(Colour-Rail NE130/Pendragon)*

Page 4 Bottom: By 1937, the new LNER B17 'Sandringham' class 4-6-0's designed by Gresley were being introduced on Marylebone services. Here is one of the 'Footballers', no.2854 'Sunderland' at Aylesbury, heading an up train of smart Gresley coaches. A fine Met-liveried coach can be seen in the bay platform behind. *(Clive Foxell Coll.)*

A list of the colour illustrations at the rear of the book is given on page 136.

(For simplicity, all forms of the Metropolitan Railway are referred to as the 'Met', of the Metropolitan & Great Central Joint Committee as the 'Joint' and from the London Passenger Transport Board to London Underground Ltd. as 'LT'.)

To Shirley and Elizabeth

First Published 2002

By Clive Foxell at 4 Meades Lane, Chesham, Bucks, HP5 1ND

Also by the author: Low Noise Amplifiers (with J. Walling)
Chesham Shuttle
Chesham Branch Album
The Story of the Met & GC Joint Line

ISBN 0 9529184 3 9

Printed by: Stanley Mason Printers Ltd.,
61 Woodside Road
Amersham, Bucks, HP6 6AA

MEMORIES of the MET & GC JOINT LINE

(THE MET & GC JOINT COMMITTEE LINE
FROM HARROW TO QUAINTON ROAD)

Dr Clive Foxell CBE FREng

Sir Edward Watkin, described in Vanity Fair, 1875: *"Above all he is a Chairman of Railways. The South-eastern, the Metropolitan and the Manchester & Sheffield lines have all placed themselves under his charge, and he rules them with a rod of iron and success that has caused him to be looked upon as a saviour of shareholders and the creator of dividends. Even his enemies who assert that he is very unscrupulous, admit that he is very clever and a very hard worker."*

ACKNOWLEDGEMENTS

One of the pleasures of writing my earlier books on the Joint has been the large number of letters that I have received from readers. In particular, they have often shared reminiscences of the line, enclosed photographs or other ephemera and mentioned other worthwhile contacts. So I thank all those that took the trouble to write to me - and buy the books! In particular, I would like to acknowledge the helpful comments by Donald Bell, Desmond Croome, Kenneth Brown, Len Bunning.

For the interviews I wish to thank many local people, especially Jean Catherine, Tony Geary, Don Grant, Ken Palmer and Iris Prior. I also believe that the photographs help to recapture the atmosphere of the Joint and here I am very pleased to acknowledge the assistance of John Parnham and Christopher Miles in New Zealand, Patrick O. Hind and Tony Newman in Canada, the late Geoff Gamble, Les Reason, and also Michael Brooks for the photographs of the late Stephen Gradidge. My sincere apologies go to those whose photographs I have been unable to contact for permission to use, or even attribute. For expert information on tickets and luggage labels I am indebted respectively to Godfrey Croughton and Chris Dickerson.

The Great Central Railway Society obviously has a strong interest in this subject and I appreciate the tremendous assistance of Richard Hardy, Michael Fish, Peter Rousselange and John Quick. Local friends, such as, Ron White (*Colour-Rail*), Ray East, John Gercken, Peter Hawkes (*Hawkes Design*), Ken Goodearl, Ron Potter, Colin Seabright and Rodney Sedgewick, have again been of great help. Equally Richard Casserley, Jim Connor of the London Railway Record, the late Tony Coldwell and *Aerofilms Ltd* kindly provided illustrations from their collections. I am also grateful for the permission of the *Railway Magazine* to use some data from early issues.

As before, the staffs of the National Monuments Record (NMR), National Railway Museum (NRM), London Metropolitan Archives (LMA), Leicestershire, Leicester & Rutland Record Office (LLRRO), Public Record Office and Westminster City Archive have been most helpful. Equally unstinting have been those of the Buckinghamshire Record Office & County Museum for access to the County Record Office Collection (BCRO), also the Brent and the Harrow Record Offices, as well as my local libraries.

A particular pleasure in producing this book has been the chance to work again with Peter Green, the railway artist who created the memorable posters for 'Steam on the Met', and who realised the evocative painting of Rickmansworth used for the front cover. Finally, I am indebted to Archie Eager and his printers for their efforts, also Len Bunning, Peter Cowan, Ken Goodearl and Elizabeth Foxell for checking the final draft. Nevertheless, in spite of all this help any mistakes that have occurred are entirely my responsibility.

Clive Foxell Autumn 2002, Chesham

PREFACE & CONTENTS

The use of *'Memories'* in the title is somewhat of a licence to include a motley collection of recollections and images to mark the centenary of the 'Joint' line. To claim 100 years is not unreasonable if one recalls that the first GCR train over the Met metals ran in 1898 and their Joint agreement came into effect in 1906. My previous books about the Met & GC Joint Committee line have covered the basic history, and, it could be thought unnecessary to repeat the exercise. However, I have been intrigued by a number of 'loose ends' which have merited further research and also become increasingly aware that the stories of those who were actually involved in operating the Joint reveal the practical and human side of this distinctive and heterogeneous railway, only some 48½ miles long. Equally, I have been able to locate a number of relevant photographs, mainly unpublished, with which to illustrate the story. Therefore in many ways this is a companion to my 'The Story of the MET & GC Joint Line', but it is self-contained and I have attempted to cast a fresh light on an idiosyncratic, but much-loved railway line, that is still evolving and may yet regain its access to the north.

CONTENTS

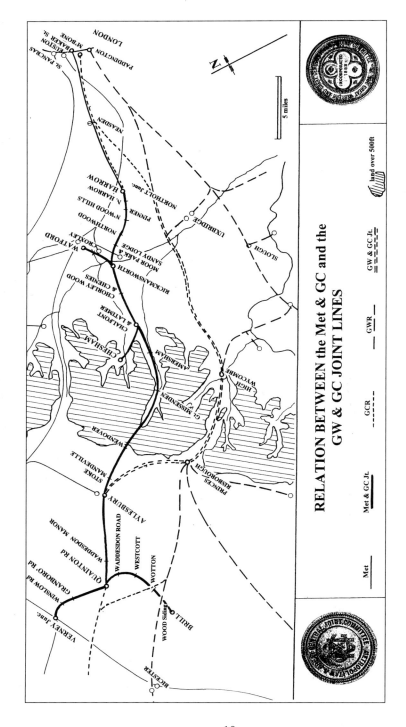

RELATION BETWEEN the Met & GC and the
GW & GC JOINT LINES

Met ——   Met & GC Jt. ——   GCR - - - -   GWR — —   GW & GC Jt. = = = =

land over 500ft

5 miles

N

INTRODUCTION

The creation of the Metropolitan and Great Central Joint Committee in 1906, to manage the operations over the line between Harrow and Quainton Rd., marked the end of Sir Edward Watkin's attempt to create a rail link to the Continent. Born in 1819, he was brought up in a prosperous family cotton business that was trading on an international basis and which increasingly depended on fast, reliable transport. Inevitably the wider opportunities demonstrated by the nearby Liverpool & Manchester Railway, opened in 1830, impressed him and by 1845, he had risen sufficiently by his own efforts to embark on a railway career as Secretary of the strategic Trent Valley Rly. His negotiations for its sale to the larger London & Birmingham Rly. impressed even the latter's buccaneering manager, Capt. Mark Huish who, recognising a like spirit, recruited him to the emerging LNWR. However, those very qualities of acumen, charisma and a mix of charm and aggression meant that Watkin had to be his own master. Following major overseas, activities he returned to Britain, imbued with the possibilities for international trade and in 1853, joined the Manchester, Sheffield & Lincolnshire Rly.(MS&LR) to be their General Manager and, after a characteristic battle of wills, Chairman in 1864.

Watkin's forceful character brought him to the attention of many beleaguered railway companies and soon he was appointed as chairman or director to many boards. Either by accident or design, these included - as well as the MS&LR - the Metropolitan, South Eastern(SER), East London, Aylesbury & Buckingham (A&BR) railways and Chemins de Fer du Nord. Becoming a francophile, Watkin conceived the possibility of linking these via a Channel Tunnel to create a railway between Manchester and Paris. This motivation led him to extend the MS&LR south to join the A&BR, which was acquired by the Met as part of its western extension from Baker Street. With his hold over the SER, the way was now clear to Folkestone and, under his Chairmanship of the Channel Tunnel Co., boring of the tunnel advanced about 1,800 metres from both coasts.

However, with the completion of his dream almost in sight, in 1894 Watkin became ill and with his powers of leadership failing, the scheme disintegrated. In particular, his trusty lieutenants, Pollitt (General Manager of the MS&LR, becoming the Great Central Rly. in 1897) and Bell (GM of the Met), became bitter enemies and their disagreements over sharing the Met line into London led to chaos. This was only resolved after they both retired, for by that time their antagonism was obviously counter-productive as the GCR had out-manoeuvred the Met by forming a joint company with the GWR and thereby obtained an easier

3rd Duke of Buckingham
& Chandos

Sir Harry Verney

John Bell

Sir Edward Watkin

William Pollitt

Robert Selbie

Sir Sam Fay

CREATORS OF THE 'JOINT' LINE

alternative route into Marylebone. Therefore, the Met was forced to sign a similar 'Joint' agreement in 1906 to share their own line with the GCR. The next generation of managers, Robert Selbie (Met) and Sam Fay (GCR), adopted a more pragmatic approach to their association and although they remained sensitive to delineation issues, both were more interested in increasing overall traffic. These more stable classic years continued through the railway grouping in 1923, when the LNER absorbed the GCR, and also after the Met reluctantly bowed to the might of London Transport in 1933. Indeed the new partners continued the Joint Agreement until the 1948 nationalisation of the railways. Even with the advent of BR, the same framework continued, but major changes followed with electrification of the Met in 1961, then DMU services from Marylebone replacing steam in 1966 and their subsequent successful privatisation as Chiltern Railways. They still share tracks and a contractual relationship continues between Chiltern Railways and LUL today. Looking to the future, the current proposals imply that the Met/LUL will be limited to services only for Watford and Uxbridge, whilst an expanding Chiltern Railways and possibly CrossRail will serve the 'Extension'.

This book reviews the development of the Joint line and considers some of Watkin's original intentions. During the heyday of the expansion of the railways in the 19th century, proposals for new lines grew at an enormous rate. Apart from absorbing the efforts of vast numbers of promoters, surveyors, engineers, lawyers and parliamentarians, the crucial elements were the acquisition of the necessary land/rights of way and the finance to build the lines. Watkin was very active in all aspects and had two reasons for promoting extensions to his empire. Firstly, a straightforward strategic branch, which would often be pursued in a surreptitious manner in order to avoid alerting the competition or increasing the asking price for the land. Alternatively, with suitable publicity it might be a ploy to distract or frighten away competitors from a desirable area.

In that Watkin had to force a way for his north-south railway between the territories of the existing major players i.e. GWR, LNWR, Midland Rly. etc., he was often 'caught in the 'crossfire' between them of promoted railways. However, Watkin himself was a master of such dealings and often used such 'phantom' schemes as a tactic to encourage recalcitrant partners. But inherently Watkin liked to associate himself with other relevant schemes in order to keep as many of his options open. In my previous book, I dealt with some examples of his varied approach, such as the erstwhile extension of the Wotton Tramway to Oxford as the O&AT and the proposed branch from Rickmansworth to High Wycombe. In later chapters here, I describe some of the more intriguing of his schemes which, if they had not been aborted, would have produced a completely different 'Joint' railway.

ooooo000ooooo

𝕸etropolitan and 𝕲reat 𝕮entral 𝕵oint 𝕮ommittee.

MINUTES of MEETING of OFFICERS of the Great Central and
Metropolitan Companies, held at 32, Westbourne Terrace,
Paddington, on February 8th, 1906.

Sanctioned by Directors.
3rd May 1906 except
Minutes. 13, 19. 23. 40 & 41.

Present :

Confirmed by
Officers 30/6/06

On behalf of the Great Central Company.	On behalf of the Metropolitan Company.
Mr. R. HAIG BROWN,	Mr. H. B. PALMER,
,, C. T. SMITH,	,, W. H. BROWN,
,, W. CLOW,	,, J. H. FINLAYSON,
,, J. LEES,	,, F. CROCKER.
,, R. PASS,	
,, W. A. ROBINSON,	
,, H. M. BOWDEN,	
,, G. E. WARBURTON.	

1.——Joint Staff.

It was agreed to recommend, in view of the fact that the present
staff on the Joint Line were all Metropolitan servants, it would, to enable
the appointments to be equalised, be necessary for the Great Central to
fill up whatever vacancies may occur until such time as the nominations in
each grade by each Company are equal; subsequent appointments to be
afterwards made alternately in grades by the two Companies; men
nominated for positions as station-masters by either Company to be subject
to the approval of the other.

The principle above referred to is that generally adopted in joint
arrangements.

The Metropolitan representatives stated that at Aylesbury, the Station
being joint with the Great Western, the above arrangements would not
altogether apply.

THE JOINT AGREEMENT OF 1906

The main provisions of the agreement signed in 1906 for the GCR to share the Met Extension reflected the history of the lack of trust between the two parties and fell into two broad categories. Firstly, the principles of ownership, management and finance were as follows:

Met & GC Joint Committee to control the line from Harrow South Junction to Quainton Road and Verney Junction, including the Brill branch, but excluding that to Uxbridge.

Met to lease the above lines to the Joint for 999 years at £44,000 p.a. and a new double track that they will build from Neasden to Harrow for 999 years at £22,000 p.a.

GC to guarantee Met receipts for Baker Street - Harrow and GC fares not to be less than the Met.

Met and GC to have equal shares of profit, new investment and staff. Management via a Joint Committee of Principals supported by a Committee of Officers. In this, the main functions (i.e. management, finance etc.) to alternate between the partners every 5 years and most operations to be shared or allocated on an agreed basis.

Secondly, these measures had to be implemented operationally in a transparent manner, demonstrating that there was no bias towards one party or the other. This led to a bureaucratic environment that probably only worked because of the goodwill of the staff involved. The complexity of these arrangements (which changed responsibilities every 5 years!) is shown by the following précis of the instructions for the period 1932-1936, issued on 4th December 1931 by George Hally (Traffic Manager and Chief Mechanical Engineer of the Met) on passing control to the LNER.

1. *PAYBILLS to be forwarded as follows:*
            operating staff to District Superintendent LNER
            passenger commercial staff to District Passenger Manager LNER
            goods commercial staff to District Goods Manager LNER
2. *RELIEF STAFF, applications for operating staff to the District Inspector and for commercial staff as above.*
3. *LOST PROPERTY from Met trains to be forwarded to the Lost Property Office, Baker Street and special value items to the Traffic Manager's Office, Baker Street. All items found on LNER trains, those found on the premises and unclaimed items must be forwarded to the Lost Property Depot, Marylebone.*

4. *UNCLAIMED TRAFFIC on the Joint to be reported to the Goods Manager LNER, except those received via the Met route which must be reported to the Met Commercial Manager.*

5. *REPORTING OF ACCIDENTS. All cases must be immediately reported to the District Manager LNER and the Traffic Manager Met.*

6. *PASSENGER CLAIMS, COMPLAINTS Etc. Those relating to traffic between stations on the Joint send to the District Passenger Manager LNER. Those arising with traffic on the Met or beyond to the Met Commercial Manager.*

RATES FOR PASSENGER TRAIN TRAFFIC ie perishable merchandise, horses & carriages etc between stations on the Joint from the Passenger Manager LNER.. Between Joint stations and Met stations or beyond Finchley Road or Baker Street from the Commercial Manager Met. Between Joint Stations and all others by other routes from the Passenger Manager LNER.

GOODS TRAIN TRAFFIC. Claims & compensation arising on Merchandise & Live Stock between Joint Stations and Met stations or beyond Finchley Road and Farringdon & High Holborn to the Commercial Manager Met. For traffic between Joint Stations and all others via Aylesbury, Verney Junction, Quainton Road, Harrow South Junction and Marylebone claims to District Goods Manager LNER..

RATES FOR GOODS TRAIN TRAFFIC. For between Joint stations apply to Goods Manager, Rates & Charges Section, LNER.. For rates between Joint and Met stations (including beyond Finchley Road or Farringdon & High Holborn) apply to the Commercial Manager Met. For between Joint stations and all others via Verney Junction, Quainton Road, Aylesbury, Harrow South Junction and Marylebone apply to the Goods Manager, Rates & Charges Section LNER.

7. *ROUTES - GOODS TRAIN TRAFFIC (exclusive of Chesham).*

Unconsigned Goods, Mineral & Livestock must be sent during the following months in accordance with the LNER's routing instructions:-

1932 January, March, May, July, September, November and so on until February 1937. The Met's months for such traffic will be:-

1932 February, April, June, August, October, December and so on until January 1937. Consigned traffic must be sent by the route indicated on the Consignment Note.

8. *DEMURRAGE. Forms rendered to the Met must continue to be used and no alteration made in the existing practice of rendering monthly returns to the District Goods Manager LNER. All disputes to be referred to the Commercial Manager Met.*

9. *DAILY STOCK RETURNS. In respect of all merchandise & coaching stock traffic on the Met's route to the Traffic Manager Met. Coaching stock returns for Joint local traffic and by all other routes other than the Met must be sent to the District Passenger Manager LNER. The Met. & GC Joint Crane will be under the control of the LNER..*

10. *PARCELS IN HAND or which cannot be delivered must be reported immediately to the District Passenger Manager LNER for instructions on disposal, except that received by the Met's route which must be reported to the Commercial Manager Met.*

11. *BREAKDOWNS & OBSTRUCTIONS. Each Company will clear its own breakdowns, but in serious cases the assistance of both Companies must be called for.*

12. *PROSECUTIONS will be undertaken by the LNER and all irregularities must be reported to the District Officers of the Department concerned, LNER, with the exception that prosecutions arising from ticket irregularities must be reported to the Passenger Manager LNER.*

13. *TRAFFIC NOTICES will be issued by the LNER.*

14. *JOINT PUBLIC TIME TABLES will be issued by the LNER and the Advertising Manager LNER will arrange distribution. Unsold copies must be parcelled and returned to him.*

15. *CLOTHING will be supplied by the Met.*

16. *PASSES. Applications must be addressed to the respective District Officers of the LNER mentioned in paragraph 1.*

17. *EXCURSION ARRANGEMENTS between Joint stations will be undertaken by the LNER and through the District Passenger Manager. Similar arrangements to or via LNER or Met stations will be made by the respective Companies.*

18. *SUPPLY OF PASSENGER ETC TICKETS. Will continue to be supplied by the Met. Season Tickets will be supplied by the Met & LNER on similar lines to those already in operation.*

19. *ACCOUNT MATTERS. The Met will keep the accounts for the JOINT. The LNER will authorise all credit accounts and applications must be sent to their respective District Managers.*

20. *STORES, BILLBOARDS & STATIONERY will be supplied by the LNER.*

21. *GOODS & PARCELS CARTAGE will be controlled by the LNER.*

22. *TENANCIES FOR CAB & OMNIBUS STANDINGS will be conducted by the LNER.*

23. *HARROW SHUNTING ENGINE will be provided by the LNER on and from January 1st ,1932*

24. *STORAGE SPACES & TENANCIES IN GOODS YARDS. Letting at Great Missenden and stations south thereof, including the Watford Line to be dealt with by the Commercial Manager Met. At stations north of Great Missenden they will be dealt with by the District Goods Manager LNER and the Mineral Manager LNER in respect of Coal Class Tenancies.*

25. *COAL, COKE & PATENT FUEL communications to the Mineral Manager LNER in respect of traffic between JOINT stations and to/from such stations via Aylesbury, Verney Junction, Quainton Road and Harrow South Junction. In respect of traffic between JOINT Line Stations and the Met and lines beyond via Finchley Road, they must be addressed to the Commercial Manager Met.*

26. *GENERAL. All matters in hand with the Met will be carried through until completed, but questions arising as from 1st January 1932 must be dealt with in accordance with these instructions.*

27. *PASSENGER TRAIN SERVICE & STATION AMENITIES. Matters arising from public communications or any other suggestions relating to improvements to be reported to the District Passenger Manager LNER, except as regards the Met services, which should be reported to the Traffic Manager Met*

28. *ACKNOWLEDGMENT. Please acknowledge receipt to the Traffic Manager Met*

DECEMBER 1931   *Ref: G/58428.*

So far as Aylesbury is concerned, this station is being dealt with separately and other instructions will be issued (Aylesbury was in effect a tripartite station being owned by the Met & GC Joint and the GW & GC Joint Committees).

ooooo000ooooo

17

BAKER STREET, MARYLEBONE & HARROW

Although Baker Street and Marylebone stations were not formally part of the Joint, these respective headquarters of the Met and the GCR were in another sense the most important stations to the Joint. The Joint Committee held no jurisdiction over these stations but every aspect of their operation influenced the flow of traffic over the Joint. Equally, as they were the headquarters of the partners, the location of the meetings of the controlling 'Joint Committee' and the sub-committee of the 'Officers' alternated between them.

Being the site of their respective headquarters, they became suitably impressive flagships for their companies. When Robert Selbie took over as General Manager in 1908, he launched a revitalisation of the Met, typified by electrification and the concept of MetroLand, which culminated in the rebuilding of Baker Street station in 1929 to reflect their mainline pretensions. The six sub-surface platforms dealing with the Inner Circle and Extension lines were overarched by the modern block of Chiltern Court, complete with flats, restaurant, ballroom, shops and cinema. With the addition of the Bakerloo line in 1906, Baker Street was a hive of activity, with passengers grouped round the complex destination boards or listening out for one of the stationmen. These always seemed to be tall men whose voices could carry the whole length of a platform giving in great detail the complex destinations of the approaching trains. The hubbub was increased by the noise of hundreds of coach doors being slammed shut and of the guard signalling 'all-clear', by raising the brass handle of his flag across the two wires that ran the length of the platform, to sound the electric bell near the driver.

Sir Edward Watkin had originally intended that Baker Street would also serve his London Extension of the GCR and form a gateway via his associated companies to the Continent, but practical considerations (described later) led to construction of a new terminus for the GCR at Marylebone. However, Watkin ensured that this would, in scale and architecture, rival the existing London termini of the other mainline companies. With matching hotel and other facilities, the vast overall glass roof was intended to allow for expansion, but Watkin's dreams were only partially fulfilled and just 4 platforms were ever built. Indeed, in the 1930's, it still handled less than 100 passenger trains per day, - in contrast to some 500 by Baker Street (albeit of a completely different type). Of course, there were times of intense activity such as the early morning newspaper train, peak hour commuting trains or the "Sheffield Special", but there could also be long periods of utter calm with no

In an early photograph of about 1860, a railway policeman watches the construction of Baker St. station for the new Metropolitan Rly. A wide trench has been dug for the platforms plus broad gauge tracks, and is now being covered by a brick arch to support the Marylebone Rd. The Met opened on the 10th January 1863. (*Clive Foxell Collection*)

To haul the trains for the new Met Extension service north of Aylesbury, Watkin ordered some 0-4-4T C class engines based on the design of his existing SER Q class tank locos. Here, in front of the old Baker St. North manual signal box in 1901, no.69 is about to leave for Verney Junction, 'in the middle of nowhere'.   (*R H Whitehorn*)

As part of Selbie's drive to bolster the mainline status of the Met and provide a suitable focus for MetroLand, he embarked in 1912 on an ambitious project to rebuild Baker St. station. Apart from a modified track layout and incorporation of the Bakerloo line, by 1929 it was enhanced by a new headquarters and the prestigious Chiltern Court flats.

The rebuilding of Baker St. station on such a restricted site raised the problem of servicing the new flats. To this end, a small siding (no.1) was added to the west for access. Until 1961 a Bo-Bo hauled train from Neasden brought coal and then removed the rubbish. This involved a complex shunting manoeuvre with two locos.   (LTM)

Watkin forced through the acquisition of the residential land at Marylebone needed for building his fine new GCR terminus. Here the site is being cleared, at a time in the mid-1890's, when he still hoped to link the GCR to his Met by a tunnel sweeping under the land in the middle distance. But as his health deteriorated this plan faded. *(LLRRO)*

Upon completion of the GCR London Extension, a demonstration trip was arranged for officials on the 12th February 1899. Travelling non-stop from Rugby, after sharing the Met tracks, it is seen here passing over the NLR to arrive at Marylebone at 3pm. The train is hauled by no.862, a Pollitt designed 4-4-0 class 11. *(J Parnham Collection)*

The concourse of Marylebone station in the first year of the Met & GC Joint Cttee. At this time it usually had an ambience of 'cloistered calm', as the GCR expresses were still lightly loaded and commuting from Bucks was in its infancy. Therefore this was probably a posed picture just for publicity purposes. *(Clive Foxell Collection)*

On the 23rd July 1907, King Edward VII was conveyed by the GCR royal train to Wendover on a visit to his friend, Alfred Rothschild, at Halton. This rare picture shows it leaving Marylebone, headed by a Robinson class 8D 4-4-2 locomotive no.364, 'Lady Henderson', proudly carrying the royal 4-lamp headcode. *(GCRS)*

Another Marylebone scene at the beginning of the Joint era, with passengers leaving a new arrival, headed by a gleaming class 11 4-4-0 express engine, designed by J G Robinson. His stylish modern locos complemented the superior GCR coaches and dining cars to give this late-comer to London the edge that Sam Fay needed. *(C Foxell Coll.)*

By 1919, the crack 3.15pm GCR express train from Marylebone to Manchester had become known as the 'Sheffield Special'. As the loading was usually light, this example of double-heading is unusual. Both built to Robinson designs, the leading engine is no.431 a 4-4-0 'Director' class 11E, with behind a class 8B 4-4-2.*LCGB/KenNunn Coll.)*

exhaust steam, whistles or announcements - and even the stationmen seemed to speak in whispers. Indeed it was said that a London bishop, when asked for a suitable place for peaceful contemplation, suggested Marylebone station! Later, John Betjeman likened it to a provincial library lost in London. However, the goods traffic of coal, fish, timber etc went further to match Watkin's expectations, although still not quite justifying the lavish facilities provided. By contrast the goods traffic at Baker Street was small, with through GWR trains from the City to Paddington and the odd wagons bringing coal to Chiltern Court and removing its rubbish.

In more recent times, the attempts to close Marylebone by diverting traffic to Baker Street foundered on the impracticality of coping with more trains at this station. Ironically, this ultimately led to the resurgence of Marylebone under Chiltern Railways, to the point where it is busier than ever and plans are afoot to add two more platforms, as services for both old joint lines are expanded.

North from Baker Street on the Met, Finchley Road was also of importance to the Joint, as Watkin had quickly established an interchange facility here with the Midland Railway which coal trains from the north began to use this 1880. With the construction of Watkin's tower at Wembley, the GCR became apprehensive about the consequent congestion of the Met tracks and in 1901, the Met was forced to provide dedicated tracks for the GCR trains to run to Harrow. Next, Neasden was the site of their respective engine sheds, with that of the Met on the east side and the GC/LNER to the west side. Following the acquisition of the Met by LT in 1933, most of their steam engines for use beyond Rickmansworth were transferred to the LNER in 1937.

The real Joint tracks began at Harrow South box and so the first true station of the Joint was Harrow on the Hill, opened by the Met in 1880. It was rebuilt with four tracks to accommodate the GCR in 1907 and again in 1938 by Frank Pick in the LT house-style, with an LT 'circle & bar' logo above the LNER 'lozenge' to represent its Joint status. From the start, this was an important station to both companies because it generated significant passenger and goods traffic, was an attractive interchange point and formed a junction which effectively controlled the entry to the Joint. It became a very attractive station for a large commuter catchment area and the Met sought to limit the ability of the GCR to structure their fares to 'cream off' Met customers. Also from the passenger's perspective, Harrow provided a convenient place to change for a myriad of destinations (ie the City, Baker Street or Marylebone, Uxbridge, Watford, Chesham, Aylesbury and the north of England) and, even for the same destination, to play the options of joining fast or slow trains. Experienced commuters would swap trains at Harrow knowing the niceties of the timetables, plus the factors that would allow a specific

The driver and guard look across as Met no.34 class B 4-4-0T hauls a down train past Willesden for Harrow. The class B engines had rather larger side tanks than the earlier versions and it is hauling a primitive 4-wheel coach amidst a rake of the 8-wheel rigid types. The picture must easily pre-date the sale of the loco in 1905.   *(NRM/LPC)*

Also at Willesden about the same time, but on the GCR tracks, no.874 heads a down express of just 4 coaches. The class 11 4-4-0 was designed for the opening of the London line by the enigmatic Harry Pollitt, son of the Managing Director. With the creation of the GCR, the coach livery became brown with French grey upper panels. *(Real Photos)*

Neasden Met station in 1896, when it was still set in open countryside and before the GCR tracks were added in the foreground. From the smoke-filled tunnels under London, a Met train heads for Harrow with a classic Beyer-Peacock designed class A tank engine (no.14, hauling a mixed rake of 8 and 4 -wheel Ashbury coaches. *Brent Archive)*

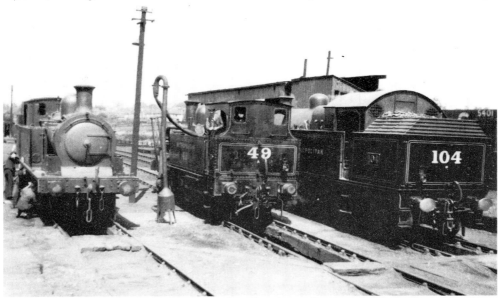

Neasden Met loco shed about 1934, before the absorption into LT had taken full effect and the majority of engines transferred to the LNER in 1937. On the right, the fitters are working on the coupling rod of no.93 (an F class 0-6-2T), whilst in the centre sits no.49 (an A class 4-4-0T) and to the right, no.104 (an H class 4-4-4T). *(H C Casserley)*

Neasden power station in 1935 dominates one of the two Met Peckett 0-6-0T's, largely acquired to share the shunting at Harrow yard with the GCR under the Joint Agreement. Between their 5 year stints, they were either used for short trips from Neasden, or put in store! Met no.101 became LT no.53, seen above in a interim LT livery. *(H C Casserley)*

A late-1940's view of Neasden (LNER) shed from the top of the coaling tower. Until 1944, Matthew Robinson (Dist. Loco. Supt. and son of 'JG') had the front office near the clock. In the foreground are a row of A5's and from l to r: a breakdown train; grounded Met electric & GCR coaches; a K3; D11; Met tank & extreme rt.a B7. *(GCRS)*

Watkin was a francophile and became so impressed by the Eiffel Tower that he started to build a (higher!) version at Wembley. However, after reaching the first stage the public interest faded. A branch was built to carry materials for the construction and this was subsequently used for electrification experiments. *(C Foxell Collection)*

A view that reflects the decline of Watkin. At Wembley his tower is about to be demolished, whilst over the horizon, his Met line is in dispute with his GCR over sharing access to London. To apply pressure, the GCR has joined the GWR to build a bypass to the Met, seen in the foreground. It was completed in 1905. *(Clive Foxell Coll.)*

One of the first Met locos, a condensing A class 4-4-0T no.2 was built in 1864 and initially carried the name 'Mars'. The engine was built by Beyer-Peacock some 8 years before the Met Extension reached Harrow and it is seen there running light near the temporary Station Road bridge. The loco was scrapped in 1907.   *(J E Connor/ LRR)*

In the early 1900's, cabs were added to some of the class A tank engines to give some protection to the crews when exposed to the elements over the Chiltern Hills. This picture shows loco no.3 approaching Harrow on the Hill with a down train of 4 and 8 - wheel rigid Ashbury coaches, commonly known as 'bone shakers'.   *(NRM/ Rhodes)*

An up GCR express from Manchester, just after passing Harrow, with a rake of their sumptuous clerestory coaches hauled by a 'bogie pom-pom' class 11B - one of the fine Robinson designs that were to sustain the GCR. The scene dates from after it was built in 1903, to 1904 when this engine was damaged in the Aylesbury crash. *(R H N Hardy)*

A calm picture of Harrow on the Hill station after it was rebuilt in 1908 to handle the growing traffic from the Extension, the recent Uxbridge branch and electrification. Inevitably a row developed between the partners of the Joint as to who should pay for the work, as the GCR felt that this primarily benefited the Met! *(Peter Rousselange/GCRS)*

The point of the change over to steam traction moved north as the electrification of the Met progressed under Selbie. Some of the first electric locomotives were the Bo-Bo's supplied by BTH in 1908, which served until replaced in 1921-2. Here, BTH no.15 waits in the layby south of Harrow near the manual coaling stage. *(R J Greenaway Coll.)*

A row of shops now covers Station Road bridge at Harrow on the Hill in 1938, whilst in the foreground, the regular down train of empty milk tank wagons are being returned to Dorrington, in Shropshire, via Woodford Halse. The engine is an ex-GCR 4-4-0 'Improved Director' named 'Jutland' and now an LNER class D10. *(GCRS/Coles)*

Harrow had been rebuilt in LT style in 1938 and, later in 1948, a Watford-bound T stock multiple-electric waits at no.4 platform. The 'away' will be given by the guard placing the brass handle of his green flag across the overhead bell wires. In the background, on platform no.6, friends are bidding farewell to a LNER express.   *(POH/Eric Johnson)*

The view south from Roxborough Road bridge towards Harrow on the Hill station on the 3rd September 1966, as BR(M) class 5 4-6-0 no.45292 passes underneath with the last through passenger service from Marylebone to Nottingham. The smokebox of the engine carries the appropriate chalked message 'The Last Day - Great Central'.   *(B H Jackson)*

train to depart first. The public address system was woefully inadequate and the problem was the need to read the relevant indicator board and signals across several platforms and sprint across via the bridge or subway. However this latter manoeuvre was made hazardous by the loaded barrows that used the subway to move goods to the parcels office on the south side of the station and post bags to the Post Office to the north side. It also became particularly unpleasant when fish boxes (re-used till they fell apart) were being moved through the confined subway!

In practice freight traffic had grown, with the development of the Harrow area, to the extent that the goods yard had to be enlarged and the partners in the Joint fought to obtain their fair share of this business. Initially they agreed to handle the goods on alternate days, but this proved impractical and it was changed to periods of 5 years. For their period of duty, the Met bought two 0-6-0 Peckett tank engines, which remained virtually unused when the GCR/LNER operated the yard!

However, the main operational concern was over the ability to influence the Harrow signal boxes, which largely controlled the often conflicting flow of Met and GCR traffic over the Joint line. The main bone of contention was over the crucial Met Harrow South box at the entrance to the Joint and it took much argument by the GCR before it was designated a Joint box in 1907. However, in reality, final control lay in the hands of the signalmen and, as it had been agreed that Joint staff could only come from the partners and that an equal balance should be maintained overall, this could lead to local favouritism towards trains of one of the companies. The other Harrow signal boxes were also strategically placed to preferentially juggle the interlacing of fast, stopping and goods trains of both companies. Indeed sometimes relations between staff of different allegiances deteriorated to the point where they would no longer speak directly to each other!

However at the level of the Joint Committee, the allocation of ticket revenues at Harrow was the main concern and, starting in 1904, with over £1million in dispute, it remained an ongoing source of friction.

oooo0000oooo

MISSING LINK - MARYLEBONE TO BAKER St.

By 1890 Watkin could contemplate with much satisfaction the progress on his railways from Manchester to Paris. The MS&LR were planning their extension to the south to meet the A&BR at Quainton Road, newly acquired and upgraded by the Met, who themselves were completing their line from London to Aylesbury. Impressed by the new Eiffel Tower in his beloved Paris, Watkin started to build a similar tower - but taller - beside the Met at Wembley! To the south of London, the SER was ready to link with his Channel Tunnel, now under construction at Folkestone and Calais, where it joined the Chemins de Fer du Nord for Paris. All that seemed to remain to complete the trans-european railway was the small matter of how the MS&LR trains would cross London.

However, as with many of the details of Watkin's grand schemes, closer scrutiny revealed major practical problems. In this case, Watkin assumed that the MS&LR trains would run on the Met to Baker Street station, thence around the Inner Circle, and an agreement giving the MS&LR running powers over the Met from Quainton Road through to Baker Street was made in 1890. After strong operational objections from those actually involved, even Watkin had to admit that Baker Street could not cope with such an increase in traffic on such a restricted site. Much to the pleasure of John Bell (now, Chairman of the Met), Watkin agreed to allow the MS&LR trains from the north to terminate at a separate new station at Marylebone. But in the plans put forward for the 1892 session of Parliament, he made sure that they included a link line from this station to the Met (Inner Circle) line just west of Baker Street station. However, by now Watkin's two henchmen, Bell of the Met and Pollitt of the MS&LR, were at loggerheads. They had been rivals since the time when they both worked in the MS&LR and now each saw a joint or shared line as forcing one of them to bow to the other - with the consequent possible loss of their job. This intransigence was allowed to flourish as Watkin's health waned and Bell wanted to impose such onerous charges and restrictions on MS&LR trains using Met tracks that, by the time the requisite Bill for Marylebone was given the Royal Assent in 1893, the 'link' had been quietly dropped. Later Watkin vaguely mentioned a separate underground railway for the MS&LR under London, but by now he was quite ill and in 1894 had to relinquish all his chairmanships.

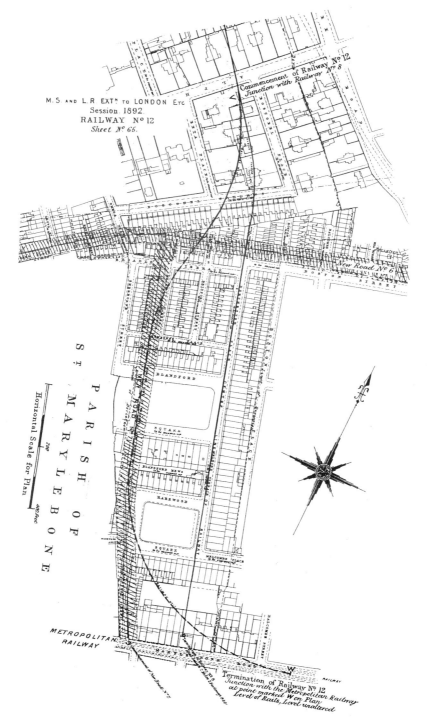

M.S. AND L.R. EXTN TO LONDON ETC
Session 1892.
RAILWAY No 12
Sheet No 66.

Commencement of Railway No 12
Junction with Railway No 8

New Road No 6

PARISH OF MARYLEBONE

St

Horizontal Scale for Plan

BLANDFORD

SQUARE

BLANDFORD MEWS

HAREWOOD

SQUARE

METROPOLITAN
RAILWAY

Termination of Railway No 12
Junction with the Metropolitan Railway
at point marked W on Plan
Level of Rails, Level unaltered

35

Nevertheless, those plans of 1892 reveal an intriguing picture of what might have been. Firstly, one is struck by the vast number of slum properties that were to be demolished to make way for the grand new Marylebone station. Imposed on this were to be two new roads (north/south no.6: Rossmore Rd. and east/west no.7: Harewood Ave.). No doubt limited by the position of the nearby Regent's Canal, the MS&LR rail link to the Met would have diverged from the mainline into Marylebone no.8, to the west via a line (no.12). At the new Rossmore Rd. bridge the link line no.12 would have descended underground at a gradient of 1 in 68.4, employing 'cut and cover' tunnelling beneath the new Harewood Ave. Then, after swinging east on a curve of about 520 ft radius, line no.12 would pass under the forecourt of the station to join on the level the existing Met lines at a rail depth of 23 ft below ground level, just short of the west end of Baker Street station.

One suspects that this junction would have proved the fundamental flaw in his grand concept because of the significant differences between the minimal Met loading gauge and that of the new GCR. Watkin seems to have overlooked this point and it did not arise until about 1897, when Bell was pestered by Pollitt of the MS&LR about access to the Met system. Pollitt started sending almost daily letters to Bell requesting details of the Met loading gauge, gradients and track curvature from Quainton Road to the City. Bell delayed his replies whilst seeking the facts from W. H. Gates, his Resident Engineer at Neasden, and, anticipating the embarrassing answers, tried to find out the comparative figures for other railways! But these confirmed the 'switchback' nature of the Met and that, although track could be lowered at bridges on the Extension to increase height clearances and meet MS&LR needs, it would be impracticable to accommodate their trains in the underground section. A reproduction of the drawing of 2/6/1897 (LMA Acc. 1297 MET 709) submitted to Watkin, showing the loading gauges (guage!) for the various sections of the Met, marked on the original with red ink to show the "outline of the MS&LR standard loco", is reproduced on the next page.

Watkin attempted to revive the original proposal by suggesting that the MS&LR could construct a larger tunnel for its trains, beneath that of the Met, in order to traverse London. However, by that time his big dream was fading, for the other crucial link in his railway to Paris, the Channel Tunnel, had been effectively blocked by nervous British politicians and the Army, and thus his GCR express trains were destined not to thunder under London on their way to the South.

ooooOOOOOoooo

METROPOLITAN RAILWAY.

LOADING GUAGE.

Scale, ½ in to 1 Ft

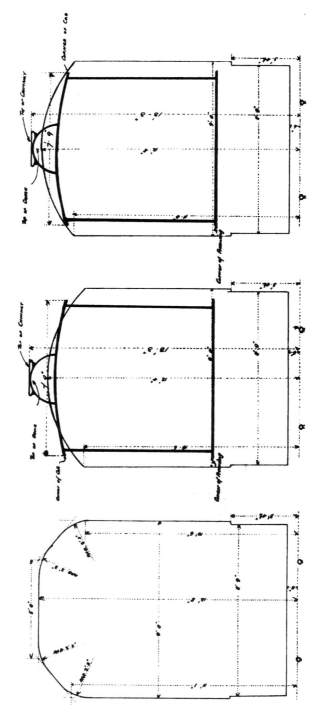

INNER CIRCLE
&
WIDENED LINES.

FINCHLEY ROAD
TO
BAKER STREET.

FINCHLEY ROAD
TO
CHESHAM.

OPERATING THE JOINT

As both the Met and the GCR had to share the line from Harrow South Junction to Quainton Road, the actual operation over these 48½ miles was always a problem due to congestion. Apart from the basic difficulty of sharing of the double tracks, matters were further complicated by the accuracy of the time that trains were presented at Quainton or Harrow, the different performance of the various trains and motive power and the contrary operating cultures of the two companies.

From the start of GCR trains using the route to Marylebone in 1899, the insertion of their northern expresses at unpredictable times into the schedule of the denser and slower Met suburban & goods services created mayhem, and thus much acrimony between the two companies. For without any overall control, decisions on pathing largely rested with the individual signalmen – and it was inevitable that company loyalties became the deciding factor when there was a conflict between the movements of Met and GCR trains. Given the antagonism of Pollitt (GCR) and Bell (Met), the disputes escalated until relations were near breaking point. Unfortunately, it took a terrible accident near Aylesbury Station in 1904 to bring realisation to the two companies that a pragmatic working arrangement had to be agreed. This crash, in which a down GCR express took the sharp reverse curve into Aylesbury at excessive speed, derailed and was then hit by the next up express, revealed serious deficiencies in the practices of both companies. Eased by changes in the leadership of both sides this belatedly led to an agreement in 1906 to operate the shared tracks through a Met & GC Joint Committee. Although the formal agreement reflected an equal partnership, with alternating senior managers and the staff employed by the Joint, in practice the GCR, with fewer trains running on an infrastructure of Met origins, was made to feel the junior partner.

It can be questioned as to why the GCR did not make more use of the Joint line. Here we need to remember that earlier, Pollitt of the GCR felt that Bell was trying to extract too high a price from him for the privilege of sharing the Met tracks. So in order to put pressure on the Met, Pollitt came to an agreement with the GWR (enemies of the Met) to support building a joint avoiding line that would enhance the GWR route to Birmingham and also provide the GCR with an alternative path to their new terminus at Marylebone. When construction of this competitor started the Met was forced to compromise, but with the 1906 Agreement they were able to obtain a commitment from the GCR to at least some ongoing use by their trains of the new Met & GC Joint Committee line.

As the GCR already had a similar agreement with the GWR for the GW & GC Joint line, this meant that they now had two routes from the north into their palatial new London terminus at Marylebone. The line shared with the Met was shorter by 5 miles, but was a 'serpentine switchback' compared with the more gently graded GW option. So whilst the GCR flagship expresses used both routes, more were scheduled via the GW. Also the majority of burgeoning GC goods traffic used this line because of the provision of passing loops, long refuge sidings and avoiding interference from Met trains. Ironically, as the Met and GWR actively developed their suburban passenger and goods services on their respective joint lines, it was the GCR who were squeezed, in spite of offering a higher quality service. So, having a half share in both of the routes proved to be less satisfactory than complete control over one – although the route diversity was useful for coping with engineering work or football trains, excursions and other specials.

Another reason for the apparent dominance of the Met, in what was nominally a joint line, was the reluctance of the GCR (and then the LNER) to fund their share of the growth in the Joint by supporting the Met's capital expenditure on the infrastructure for MetroLand. The steady growth of this commuter traffic received a substantial boost with the opening of the Watford branch in 1925 and the consequent electrification to Rickmansworth. With track capacity now near its limit, the Met introduced more electric multiple units and built a burrowing junction at Harrow north in order to avoid the conflicting movements arising from the Uxbridge branch trains. Also, in order to reduce their occupation of the Joint line Met goods trains were lengthened, together with the relevant sidings, albeit only being able to cope with 40 loaded wagons.

However, the fundamental problems remained and not all were attributable to the Met, for with only 4 platforms at Marylebone serving both Joint lines, delays were inevitable at peak times to those trains entering the Joint at Harrow South. Equally at the other end of the Joint, the GCR/LNER trains did not always keep to the precise timing needed to interlace with the Met 'all stations' slow schedules. Nevertheless, the tortuous nature of the Met route plus the speed restriction at Rickmansworth, compounded by the track occupation by their steam/electric traction changeover at this point, frustrated the Marylebone trains. The other annoying feature of Met practice was that, due to the need to switch-off power to the track at night for maintenance purposes, no electric stock movements were possible. This created even more traffic during the busy periods and to improve stock availability, a spare set of multiple T stock was kept overnight at Watford, together with a reserve set of Dreadnought coaches at Neasden and a spare steam engine at Rickmansworth.

The resulting difficulties with time-keeping on the Joint were continually being drawn to the attention of the management by the vociferous complaints of the passengers. Ironically, these affluent and influential commuters had been attracted to live in this area of the Chilterns by the promise of a fast and reliable train service to the City, which the partners in the Joint now found it hard to sustain.

However during the 1920's the Met also had to wrestle with the problems of increasing congestion at the southern end of the Joint nearer London. Firstly, Selbie sought to ease the bottleneck caused by the twin track tunnel between Finchley Road and Baker Street by constructing an underground link to Edgware Road that bypassed the existing route. However, safety restrictions on the use of Met compartment stock in tunnels rendered the proposal unworkable. Secondly, in spite of the new burrowing junction at Harrow north, the increasing traffic over the Joint was exacerbating the old operational difficulties of interlacing inherently different Met and (now) LNER trains. These were but some of the problems inherited by LT when they absorbed the Met in 1933. Frank Pick, the dynamic head of LT, immediately tried to apply the LT ethos of standardisation to the idiosyncratic Met and, coming to regard them with deep suspicion, replaced most of their senior management in order to accelerate integration with LT practices. Recognising the fundamental problems of congestion, but with more options open to him, he decided to reduce the Met bottleneck into Baker Street by extending the LT Bakerloo line parallel to the Met to Wembley Park and thence over the Met Stanmore branch. This was completed in 1939.

His other thrust was to streamline the operation of the Joint itself. Here he was able to use the close relationship he had established with Sir Ralph Wedgwood of the LNER over earlier collaborative projects to address the question of the troublesome Joint. First, Pick was able to shed most of the LT responsibilities for steam power by passing over most of their locomotives and operations beyond Aylesbury to the LNER in 1937. The engines were transferred to the LNER shed on the other side of the tracks at Neasden. In addition, the LNER assumed responsibility for parcels and goods operations. Now the way was clear for Pick to tackle the long-standing congestion on the Joint lines north of Harrow and, from a detailed study of train performance he had commissioned during the winter of 1933-4, it was apparent that the 23 fast LNER trains were averaging a total of some 70 mins delay per day. Whilst perhaps unsurprising for long-distance expresses, the consequential impact on the dense Met services was a total of 400 mins delay i.e. an impact factor of 5.7 times! Pick always favoured dramatic solutions and, again in consultation with Sir Ralph Wedgwood, he added to the current LT New Works Programme plans to quadruple the Joint tracks from Harrow to just beyond Rickmansworth, adding a useful passing loop at Chorleywood and improving the layout of Amersham. The overall effect would be to create four tracks from Rickmansworth to Baker Street.

Construction was started in 1938 but the outbreak of the last war delayed completion of the basic scheme until 1961. Subsequently, the London Midland Region of BR, which had inherited the Marylebone services, began to run them down to skeletal level with the intention of closing Marylebone - so the LT quadrupling scheme seemed to have been in vain! However, Chris Green of Network South East revitalised the Joint route to Aylesbury with modern DMU's and saved Marylebone. The later privatisation as Chiltern Railways is now leading to an expansion which may yet fully justify the LT work of 1961.

ooooo000ooooo

An artist's impression of the Joint 'burrowing junction' at Harrow North, from a contemporary Met publicity brochure. The train hauled by a Bo-Bo electric loco is bound for Rickmansworth, whilst beneath, a Westinghouse multiple-electric set from Uxbridge emerges bound for Harrow on the Hill station. *(Clive Foxell Coll.)*

Around 1935 at Harrow North signal box, the signalman and the duty flagman carefully watch a tank engine crossing back to the down line after a section of wrong line working. The locomotive is an ex-GCR now LNER class A5 4-6-2T no.5186.

(John Parnham)

North Harrow station was a convenient place for drivers of the Met electric locos to pause and unofficially swap driving between up and down trains. This enabled one of them to get back to the depot and home early! This 1948 picture shows Bo-Bo electric no.13 'Dick Whittington' at North Harrow on an Aylesbury train. *(POH/Eric Johnson)*

Approaching the station built of sleepers, known as North Harrow, is an LNER up Manchester-Marylebone express in 1948. Hauling a set of Gresley coaches is a freshly-painted Thompson 4-6-0 class B1 no.1186, slowing for the Harrow North junction. On the left lie the pre-war preparations for the four-tracking scheme.   *(POH/Eric Johnson)*

The more substantial Pinner station is pictured here in the early 1930's. It reflected the potential status of the village as part of MetroLand. Of interest is the Met diamond station logo on the left - soon to be replaced by LT bar and roundel.   *(NMR)*

Northwood station during the first world war and pre-electrification. With the four tracking by LT after the second war, the lines shown became the fast tracks and new ones were laid on the ground to the right of the old station for the slow traffic.

(Clive Foxell Coll.)

The four Met C class 0-4-4 tank engines were built in 1891 for their new Extension and only worked above ground. No. 69 was fitted with a larger boiler in 1903 (as a forerunner of the E class) and is seen here near Northwood in 1911, hauling a 4-wheel luggage van, Ashbury coaches and Pullman car in its original livery. *(Clive Foxell Coll.)*

The Met E class tanks were a larger version of the earlier C class and took over their duties on the Extension. Near Northwood in about 1912, no.80 E class 0-4-4T hauls a down Verney Junction train with luggage van. The condensing apparatus was about to be removed as they were rarely used underground by the Met.   *(Clive Foxell Coll.)*

Pollitt was responsible for some fine MS&LR designs, but lacked organisational ability. Above, his first 'single' 4-2-2 class 13 no. 967 is seen passing Northwood with a down train. He was 'retired' before it was completed in 1900 but the engine was soon used to head an important royal special from Marylebone.   *(David Jackson Coll.)*

The impressive looking Robinson express 4-6-0 ex-GC class 1 (but which never quite lived up to his expectations) and now a LNER class B2 no. 5427 is passing Northwood at speed with the up Wembley Cup Final special in 1938. Originally named 'City of London', the plates had been removed in the previous year. *(John Parnham)*

Northwood Hills station in the 1950's, looking north. Electrified in 1925, the forthcoming completion of the long-awaited LT four-tracking project in 1961 would create the extra fast lines on the left of the picture. The position of the small station clock over the tracks seems somewhat anomalous. *(NMR)*

During 1936, a class D11 4-4-0 no.5506 'Butler Henderson' travels through Northwood Hills station with an up mid-day train from Woodford. This was probably a return working for the earlier milk tanker train. The Robinson 'Director' class were one of his finest designs and, after grouping, the LNER ordered another two batches. *(J Parnham)*

The scene in 1960 with the replacement of the old bridge over the A404 near Northwood for the extra two tracks from Harrow to Watford South Junction.

The opportunity was also taken to widen the roadway of this notorious bottleneck.

Because of the war, the girders had lain beside the tracks since the start of the construction of the scheme in 1939. *(C R L Coles)*

In 1948 the new BR performed a series of comparative loco trials to guide their new design policy. The inconclusive mixed-traffic tests were held over the Joint in June and here the SR West Country class 4-6-2 'Bude' is accelerating near Northwood, with an LMS tender for water pick-up and a LNER Dynamometer car. *(Clive Foxell Coll.)*

The fragile timber station for Sandy Lodge golf course was built in 1910, with aid from the developers. As the Ebury estate grew under Lord Leverhulme, in 1923 it became Moor Park & Sandy Lodge and here the same structure still stands in 1950. It was to be rebuilt 10 years later in LT style as Moor Park, for the quadrupling of the track. *(NMR)*

Later in 1959, an ex-LNER 2-6-2 V2 class (now BR no.60842) heads a Nottingham up train for Marylebone through an unchanged Moor Park. After the speed restriction at Rickmansworth, such engines accelerated here and schoolboys revelled in standing on the decrepit footbridge - to be engulfed in steam, smoke and noise!   *(Stephen Gradidge)*

An ex-GCR LNER class B3/2 4-6-0 no. 6166 'Earl Haig' - stirring such memories of the first war - thunders past the new Watford Rd. signal box with an up Woodford train in 1936. The name was removed in 1943 upon rebuilding by Thompson (LNE) with a new boiler, cab, outside cylinders and valve gear so that it looked like his B1's.   *(J Parnham)*

49

HARROW TO CHESHAM & AMERSHAM

After Harrow, the line passed the large goods yard on the north side and crossed over the burrowing junction to Uxbridge, built in 1925 to ease congestion caused by the new traffic from Watford, then continued roughly straight and level towards Rickmansworth (1887). At first, the next station was beside the small, but well-established, village of Pinner and was built to the design of the Met Architect, Charles Clark, in his usual 'Extension' style as an echo of Harrow, but on a much more modest scale. Main buildings were on the up platform, built from yellow engineering bricks with awnings supported by cast iron columns. In later years, when Harrow had begun to spread to fill the intervening country, a rudimentary station with platforms and sparse shelters made from old sleepers and other spare timber (initially designated North Harrow Halt) was built in 1915 to serve the new housing estates. Originally, after Pinner the next station was at Northwood, but further MetroLand encouraged estates were developed by private builders who contributed to the construction of another intermediate (and more substantial) station to serve this area, called Northwood Hills and opened in 1933. These estates came to represent the epitome of MetroLand with its structured housing amidst a tamed landscape.

Recognising its position as serving a small town, important as much for providing a supply of gravel as for passengers, Rickmansworth station was constructed to a more generous standard in the usual Met style of brick and awnings, with offices on the up side and a subway to connect the platforms. The position on a sharp curve reflected the inability to acquire the necessary land, as much as Watkin's indecision on the route now to be taken. Later development by Lord Leverhulme between Northwood and Rickmansworth led to the introduction of another primitive timber station to serve the spacious houses on Lord Ebury's Moor Park estate and the adjacent golf course, opening in 1910 as Sandy Lodge.

Later, in 1925, delayed by the war and LNER indifference, a branch to Watford was opened and the tracks electrified from Harrow. Originally it had been intended to extend the branch to Watford High St. via a tunnel, but financial pressures and resistance from the local council forced it to be terminated by a small side road near Cassiobury Park. The branch included an intermediate station of Croxley Green and could be accessed from the Met mainline in both north and south directions, thus creating a triangular junction. Close to this, Watford South junction sidings were laid to nearby exhausted gravel pits so that Met/LT trains could use them as a waste dump. Rickmansworth was also included in this electrification and a bay was added to the up platform so that an electric 'shuttle service' could initially operate to Watford. One consequence of this electrification was that for services beyond Rickmansworth a change to steam haulage was necessary, until the later completion of electrification by LT in 1961. Whilst this was an operational inconvenience, to the observer it was a fascinating example of perfect co-ordination of drivers, guards and stationmen - all in less than three minutes! This brief pause was still sufficient for those commuters in need of refreshment to slip across into the station buffet for a quick drink, thoughtfully lined up on the bar in advance.

With the line now firmly in the country giving a substantial agricultural, goods and parcels activity plus a strong GCR/LNER presence, Rickmansworth had the ambience of a true Joint station. Milk churns stood on the platform until the late 1930's and the station bar did a good trade during breaks for the staff plus commuters, taxi drivers and workers from the goods yard.

Eventually Watkin decided to take a compromise route between the easier graded Misbourne Valley (but with more problematical landowners), that north direct to his beloved MS&LR, and that along the Chess Valley north to join his then friends of the LNWR at Tring. In doing this, he kept his options open to some extent by choosing a path between them via stations at Chorley Wood and Chalfont Road. Both station names were created by the Met: that of Chorley Wood being taken from a local village of 'Charleywood'. However, the penalty for his route was a difficult start on the sharp bend out of Rickmansworth followed by a slog up the Chilterns at 1 in 105. The stations were again of the same basic Clark design and although subways were provided, stationmen tended to cross from one to the other by nonchalantly vaulting down on to the track with one hand on the platform edge and then up again on the other side. Parcels and goods were transferred by trolleys via the sleepered crossings at the ends of the platforms - where their small wheels sometimes got stuck in the gaps!

As the name implies, Chalfont 'Road' was some way from any significant habitation but as housing grew, the name became Chalfont & Latimer (change for Chesham) in 1915. In 1889 the line was at first extended by a single track curving down at 1 in 66 along the side of the Chess Valley to swing across the river with an S-bend via two bridges into the relatively large town of Chesham. One can still enjoy much the same picturesque journey today on an LUL A60 train, past the only snow fences on their system, through delightful countryside, with trees meeting above the track to form a tunnel of green. Imagine the excitement of such a trip in the days of the steam 'Shuttle', when one of the more adventurous engine drivers was at the helm! Chesham certainly met Watkin's expectations for goods traffic but, following the cooling of relations with the LNWR, his eyes were now set on Aylesbury, and Chesham was to be relegated to branchline status when the Met reached Aylesbury in 1892 via Amersham, Great Missenden, Wendover and Stoke Mandeville. Again, standard Clark stations were built at these intermediate stations and that at Amersham became the focus for a 'new' town on the hill above the old one.

ooooo000ooooo

Metropolitan Railway Company.

INSPECTION OF

CHESHAM EXTENSION RAILWAY,

MAY 15th, 1889.

A SPECIAL TRAIN, to convey the Party inspecting the Extension, will leave BAKER STREET STATION at 11.45 a.m., on WEDNESDAY, May 15th.

A TRAIN will leave CHESHAM STATION for Rickmansworth at 11.45 a.m., to enable residents of Chesham attending the ceremony to join the Special Train.

An invitation to a Mr Rose of Waterside in Chesham to join the 'inspection' of the Chesham Extension, prior to the formal opening on the 8th July 1889. *(Jean Catherine)*

Between Moor Park and Rickmansworth, the branch to Watford was accessed via a triangular junction. Above in 1951, the morning pick-up goods emerges from Croxley tunnel, headed by an ex-GCR class 1B, later L3 & now BR no.69065. A massive 2-6-4T Robinson design using a 'Director' boiler, they became known as 'Crabs'. *(L V Reason)*

As the steam era came to an end it was inevitable that any spare engine would be pressed into service for odd duties, such as the pick-up goods. Here in 1956, an ex-Thompson LNER B1 4-6-0 no.61104 trundles across the Cassio bridge over the Grand Union canal upon leaving Watford goods yard.   *(L V Reason)*

As the Met engines that LT had retained for engineering duties began to deteriorate, they briefly tried diesels before acquiring some ex-GWR pannier tank locos. The first was GW no.7711 an 0-6-0T, here seen on trial at the LT rubbish tip just off the Watford Road junction. It was bought by LT as L90 in 1956 and withdrawn in 1961.*(L V Reason)*

Watford branch was opened on 7th November 1925 by a special train with dignitaries, including Lord Aberconway (Met) and Lord Farringdon (LNER), here seen after arrival at Watford. The other train on the left brought the local guests from Rickmansworth. The branch was formally under the control of a Met & LNER Joint Committee. *(LMA)*

Due to local opposition, Watford station was built on the outskirts. However, the Joint persisted and in 1927 acquired premises in the High Street for a more central station to be reached by an extension via a tunnel. Here is a picture of this building - lately the Empress Tea rooms - with Met posters. The plan faded and the shop is currently 'Next'.

The original Joint sign at Watford station, reflecting one of the many variations in advertising the ownership. Basically a Met diamond logo, the inspiration for 'Metro' came from the last Commercial Manager of the Met. The complexity of the name of this Watford subsidiary of the Joint led to the use of many variants. *(Philip S Evetts)*

A 1950's aerial view of Rickmansworth station. The Aylesbury direction is to the bottom of the page with a T stock multiple electric train in a siding on the left and to the right, the loco sidings with a Met tank. Watkin had been unable to buy part of Rickmansworth Park from the then Governor of the Bank of England and thus had to build the Met line around it. Beyond the curved station lie the extensive goods facilities. *(Aerofilms)*

An up GCR express approaching Rickmansworth around 1900. The photo shows how the tracks form a tightening curve as they enter the station, forcing the imposition of a speed restriction of 25mph - but often overlooked in practice! The engine is one of the Pollitt class 11A's, built by Beyer-Peacock for the new GCR 1899.   *(John Quick/GCRS)*

The same scene - but 35years later - with the classic 3 minute changeover from electric to steam power in progress at Rickmansworth. The Bo-Bo electric loco that brought the down train in has pulled forward, whilst a Met class H 4-4-4T engine no.110 now drifts up to be quickly coupled to the train and take it over the Chilterns to Aylesbury. *(H.C.C)*

The down early morning goods with no.113 leaving Rickmansworth yard for Verney Junction in 1936. The length of the train shows the growth in Met freight traffic over the Joint, to which they had responded by lengthening sidings and acquiring their massive K class 2-6-4T locomotives. These were built from war-surplus components. *(J Parnham)*

In the early 1950's, when BR(E) controlled the steam power, there was some effort to arrest the decline in services and ex-LNER A3 & V2 engines began to appear. Here a Woodford - Marylebone local (or 'Ord') with a V2 class 2-6-2 no.60879 threads its way through Rickmansworth station, with some snow still on the ground. *(Stephen Gradidge)*

The late 1950's of the BR(M) era, looking north into the curve through Rickmansworth station. On the left, an ex-LMS Fairburn 2-6-4T no.42087, waits to run back through the station to the coaling stage siding and take the next train on to Aylesbury. Meanwhile, an up multiple-electric Met T stock departs for Baker Street. *(S Gradidge)*

On Sundays the coaches of the Chesham 'Shuttle' were brought back from Neasden after cleaning. In 1959, near the end of the steam operation of the 'Shuttle', ex-LMS Ivatt 2-6-2T no.41272 pauses in Rickmansworth station with the 3-coach Ashbury set before proceeding past the new signal box to Chalfont & Latimer. *(L V Reason)*

The scene in 1931 after leaving Rickmansworth with a down Marylebone to Nottingham express hauled by 'Edwin A Beazley' class D10 no.5431 (in the shining LNER glossy black livery with red lining) plus a set of teak Gresley coaches. Such Robinson Directors continued to hold sway on the Joint right through the 1930's. *(R S Carpenter)*

The ubiquitous 9N 4-6-2 tank engines were another Robinson design, later perpetuated by the LNER as A5's; which became identified with their suburban services from Marylebone over the Joint. This photograph shows no.5170 leaving Chorley Wood in the summer of 1938 with a down train for Aylesbury. *(NRM/LPC)*

The tracks through Chorley Wood had been prepared for electrification in 1960 but any steam haulage was still being provided by a diffident BR(M). Into the station - past the original Met signal box and a ticket collector - drifts a Met train for Aylesbury hauled by an ex-LMS class 4 tank loco that had taken over at Rickmansworth. *(Stephen Gradidge)*

Around 1965, a Riddles BR Britannia class 4-6-2 no.70015 named 'Apollo' passes through Chorley Wood with an ex-Nottingham semi-fast train. By now, BR Midland Region had taken over responsibility for the old GCR line and were slowly running down services as a prelude to their attempted closure of Marylebone. *(Stephen Gradidge)*

The Met H class 4-4-4T locos handled most of the pre-war expresses for MetroLand. They were powerful, yet capable of dealing with the sharp curves of the Chesham branch. They were also quite tall and in their subsequent LNER days, the height of their dome and chimney was reduced. Here no.107 leaves Chorley Wood in 1935. *(NRM/LPC)*

In 1932, the Chalfont & Latimer (change for Chesham) station is still in open countryside and the platform awnings await extension to protect the passengers. Meanwhile, the now LNER express, the 3.20pm ex-Marylebone 'Sheffield Special' flies through in pristine condition, hauled by a Robinson Director class 4-4-0. *(Philip Evetts)*

Another LNER class A5 tank engine, arriving at Chalfont & Latimer during the early 1930's. As usual on this part of the Extension, a subway was provided for passengers and this one became a useful short-cut between the houses on either side of the line. Staff tended to use the path of sleepers across the tracks.   *(NRM/Rokeby Coll.)*

Later, in 1956 at Chalfont & Latimer station, the down Met train has just left and a Marylebone-bound semi-fast up train passes through. This is hauled by a rather grimy and nondescript ex-LNER V2 class 2-6-2 engine heading a mixed rake of Gresley and BR coaches.   *(Geoff Gamble Coll.)*

By June 1960, electrification at Chalfont & Latimer was moving towards completion, a year later. The scene shows passengers hurrying to board the 'Shuttle' for Chesham, having come from the London train that had left from the near platform. The vintage Ashbury coaches and ex-LMS Ivatt 2-6-2T were fitted for auto-working. *(R Winkworth)*

To the north beyond Chalfont & Latimer, the branch line to Chesham diverges to the right. In 1951, two small boys (not associated with the photographer!) watch an LT engineering train stationary at the obligatory warning board. The engine is ex-Met class F 0-6-2T now L49, soon to be replaced by a GW pannier tank. *(Philip Evetts/Neil Spinks)*

Watkin started the construction of the Met line from Rickmansworth to Chesham in 1889, on the assumption that he would then extend it to join his LNWR friends at Tring. This photo shows the navvies of the contractor, Firbank, excavating the chalk through the 'Baulks' on the approach to the new station, close to Chesham High Street. *(R East)*

The celebration to mark the completion of the Chesham line was held on the day of the formal 'inspection', the 15th May 1889. The festivities were arranged in the new goods shed with the inevitable champagnes, 9 courses, many speeches and two bands! After the Act for the last 71chains was ratified, the line opened on the 8th July.*(Peter Hawkes)*

MISSING LINK - CHESHAM TO TRING

While the Met headed towards Rickmansworth in the mid-1880's, Watkin was still undecided as to whether to pursue his northern objectives by proceeding either via High Wycombe, Amersham/Aylesbury or Tring. The latter could provide an easy link to the main line of the LNWR - with whom he currently had good relations - with low construction costs giving access to his beloved industrial heartlands. Instead, typically, he kept his options open, and avoiding the obvious route along the Chess valley from Rickmansworth, kept to the higher ground towards Amersham and Aylesbury before diverting from a new station of Chalfont Road to the north and the prosperous town of Chesham (with some 6,500 inhabitants), only 6 miles from Tring.

In 1884 Watkin visited Chesham, which up to now, had felt excluded from the railway age. Having been received with great enthusiasm by the townspeople, he commissioned Charles Liddell to survey a single line route down the side of the Chess Valley, capable of extension to Tring. The appropriate Met Bill was passed in 1885, authorising the Chesham Branch, and tentative agreement was reached with the LNWR to share costs for the link with Tring, in exchange for running powers for the LNWR to Rickmansworth. Watkin 'persuaded' the local people of Chesham to contribute about £2,200 towards bringing the branch from Millfields on the outskirts into the centre of the town. However, by October 1888 (on the recommendation of Liddell), he had already bought for £2,100 land on the far side of the town extending some 2-3 miles along The Vale towards Tring! During the speeches at the formal 'Inspection' of the Chesham Branch on the 15th May 1889 the intention to move forward to Tring was confirmed. The station at Chesham was laid out for such a line and even in the 1950's, the intended route beyond the town was still clearly visible. Indeed, older residents could recall piles of sleepers and other material stacked along the intended way.

However, the situation quickly changed with the loss of Watkin's friends from the LNWR Board following its financial problems, and this was replaced by his growing confidence in his alternative route via the A&BR to Quainton Road. Thus the plans for the Tring link faded, although much of the relevant land remained in the ownership of the Met and its successors until 1999.

Nevertheless, the practicality of such a link is somewhat doubtful for, although Chesham and Tring stations are roughly the same height above sea level, the hilly terrain between them would have involved more of the tortuous Chiltern 'switchbacks' that were such a feature of Watkin's empirical Met. The attached map shows the probable route of about 6 miles with several gradients of 1 in 70 and, although these would have been similar to those of the adjoining Chesham branch, it is difficult to believe that the goods trains that Watkin envisaged would have found this an attractive route.

ooooo000ooooo

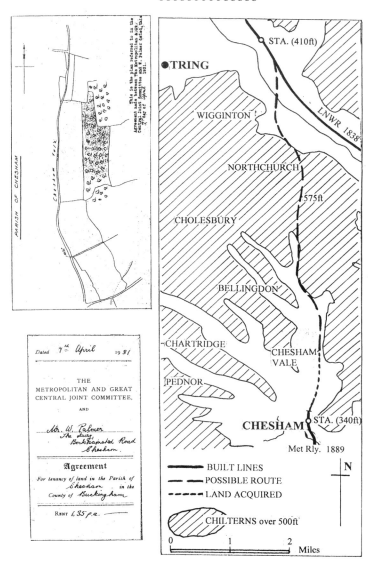

With Watkin's decision to extend the Met to Aylesbury via Chalfont Road, Chesham reverted to a branch line. Although this lowered hopes for passenger traffic, the local industries provided a healthy goods business. For example, here two horse-drawn Joint wagons are delivering cloth for Chiltern Toys in Waterside in 1923.   *(Ray East/Coll.)*

Looking along Chesham station to the north shows the direction of Watkin's proposed link to Tring. This view of 1935 is virtually unchanged since the opening, except that the faithful Met class A 4-4-0 tank engine shunting in the yard now has a cab, in order to protect the otherwise exposed crew from the weather of the Chilterns.   *(NRM/LGRP)*

In the early 1930's, the now ageing Met class E tank engines took over from the venerable Beyer-Peacock class A locos working the Shuttle. Also the original coaches were replaced by the more comfortable Dreadnoughts. No.80 is about to depart Chesham with moustached-driver William Gurney of 50 years service. *(Beryl Lammimg)*

Driver Gurney again, but this time with E class no.78 at the other end of the branch, shunting in Chalfont & Latimer yard with a distinctive Met guards van. At that time, shunting had to be fitted in between the trips with the Shuttle - often to the disadvantage of passengers! Note the then open fields now covered by housing. *(Beryl Lamming)*

A 1930's view of the Chesham Shuttle from the 'yard' side of the Chalfont & Latimer bay platform. Until 1940, the train had to be drawn out of the platform to enable the engine to run round the coaches for the return trip. But with the war, these operations were simplified by employing an auto-train formation. *(Beryl Lamming)*

The more free-spirited of the drivers of the Chesham 'Shuttle' were known to race the main line trains where they ran parallel for a time near to Raans Farm. In the mid-1950's, a Gresley V2 class 2-6-2 with a down fast-passenger train from Marylebone paces the C13 class no.67418 with the humble 'Shuttle'. *(L V Reason)*

From the first, Chesham was often the winner of the 'best gardens' competition in Met and LT days. Here in 1960, the well-known Station Master Herbert John Hudson is showing the display to a bowler-hatted judge from the headquarters at '55 Broadway'. With electrification, a new bay platform briefly replaced the garden.   *(Jean Catherine)*

This 2002 picture of Chalfont & Latimer station illustrates the current rolling stock that operate the Joint services. In the foreground is an LUL refurbished A60 multiple-electric set of 4 coaches about to depart for Chesham with the 'Shuttle'. Whilst behind a down Chiltern Railways type 165 turbo diesel is leaving for Aylesbury.   *(Clive Foxell)*

In 1903 Robinson introduced two similar designs to compare the 4-6-0 and 4-4-2 wheel arrangements. The Atlantics were very graceful and earned the nickname 'Jersey Lilies', possibly after the well-known singer Lily Langtry. The penultimate loco of this class, no.362, is seen near Amersham on a down express to Manchester.   *(H Gordon Tidey)*

Another of Richard Hardy's evocative pictures of Amersham in the 1940's, with a down Marylebone - Leicester 'all stations' train, hauled by Robinson's largest passenger loco, an ex-GCR class 9P 4-6-0. Good performers, but heavy on the coal. Then in charge of LNER no.6167 are a Neasden crew of driver Ted Mahon and fireman Ted Simpson.

A further Richard Hardy photo with the no.1 down goods train entering Amersham, before shunting into the down refuge siding. The engine is no.5341, an ex-GCR class 1 'Crab' 2-6-4T, now an LNER class L1, just beside a fine example of a Met signal at the southern end of the station.

Another typical scene at Amersham station, during 1948. The passengers on the right prepare to board an approaching down Met train for Aylesbury behind an A5 4-6-2 'Coronation' tank, which had taken over at Rickmansworth. On the opposite platform, the staff are hurrying to cross the tracks and unload any parcels. *(Alan Willmott)*

With the introduction of DMU's, the rundown of steam services over the Joint was accelerated by BR(MR). Ironically, the scrapping of steam locos resulted in a wide variety of engines being pressed into service and here in 1965, a BR Britannia no.70050 is at newly electrified Amersham with a down semi-fast for Nottingham. *(R Clarke Coll.)*

By the 1970's, the remaining Met Bo-Bo electric locos had either been preserved or relegated to engineering duties. The doyen, no.12 'Sarah Siddons', was assigned for testing brake-blocks but is here seen in Amersham with a leaf-clearing train. Subsequently it was a popular participant in 'Steam on the Met'. *(Brian Stephenson)*

The arrival of the Met Extension created easy access from London and soon mid-Bucks became a favoured place for the affluent to live. In this picture of the forecourt of Great Missenden station before the 1914-18 war, such a City commuter has just been met by his chauffeur with a solid-tyred automobile. *(Colin Seabright)*

From 1936 the new Gresley B17's began to replace the Robinson engines over the GC mainline. The war reversed the trend, but by the 1950's they were in the ascendancy. Here in Great Missenden with an up slow passenger train, is a clean B17/4 4-6-0 no. 61667 'Bradford', moving off having been given the away signal. *(L V Reason)*

AMERSHAM TO AYLESBURY & QUAINTON

Under the Joint Agreement, track maintenance was taken over from the Met by the GC north of milepost 28½, near Great Missenden. The line was relatively straight but involved an ongoing climb at 1 in 125 as far as the summit at Dutchlands (with its own signal box), some 620 ft above Baker Street. Once over the escarpment of the Chilterns, it was now downhill at 1 in 117 through Wendover station, with sidings added in 1917 to serve the Halton Light Railway. This was built by German POWs to serve the large military camp based around the sometime manor of Alfred Rothschild. The line continued downhill still at 1 in 117, through Stoke Mandeville, where the station was the largest building in the village, to the outskirts of Aylesbury some 37½ miles from London. The size of Stoke Mandeville station probably reflects the Met purchase of substantial adjoining land intended for a new works depot to replace Neasden.

Aylesbury station evolved as a result of events, rather than to a logical plan, originally much influenced by plans for the Buckinghamshire Railway. This had been floated by the 3rd Duke of Buckingham and Chandos together with Sir Harry Verney, whose enthusiasm for railways - to improve their large estates in Bucks - was in marked contrast to most other landowners, who at that time saw railways as a threat to their way of life. As a result of the involvement of the Duke with the LNWR, who earlier had built a branch to Aylesbury in 1838, they implemented the part of the Buckinghamshire Rly. plans for the Bletchley - Buckingham - Claydon - Oxford section in 1851. But soon the LNWR became disenchanted with the rest of the Duke's aspirations, so the Duke and Sir Harry took up the challenge and formed the Aylesbury & Buckingham Railway (A&BR), to run from the LNWR station at Aylesbury via Quainton Road, to be near the Wotton estates of the Duke. It would then continue on to 'Verney' Junction with the LNWR line, being built on land in the Claydon estate of Sir Harry Verney. The impoverished A&BR took eight years to build even a primitive single track light railway and they had to borrow standard gauge engines and coaches from the GWR to enable it to open in September 1868. However, they were again spurned by the LNWR who refused use of the LNWR station at Aylesbury and made the A&BR pay for the construction of Verney Junction. However, an Aylesbury terminus for a broad gauge GWR branch line from Princes Risborough had been built in 1863, and as part of their expansion plans, the GWR cannily agreed to share it with the impoverished A&BR in exchange for £28,000 towards converting the branch to narrow gauge.

Nevertheless, when Watkin (the sometime enemy of the GWR) acquired the A&BR as a way north and also extended his Met to join it at Aylesbury, this affronted the GWR, who forced the Met to build a separate station. Following a reconciliation they agreed to a joint station in 1894, but in 1904 there was the terrible crash involving GCR trains on the sharp Met curve into Aylesbury from the south. Probably due to excessive speed, there is little doubt that a contributory factor was the deteriorating relationship between the Met and the GCR, who had begun uneasily sharing the line in 1899. Indeed, it was the catalyst for the Joint Agreement of 1906, aimed at resolving such disagreements.

Now, as a consequence of this Agreement, the Met & GC and the GW & GC Joint Committees controlled the station as tripartite owners - and decisions on improving it became even more tortuous! The dangerous curve was eventually eliminated in 1907 after the usual disagreement over who should pay for it and then, after several further years of 'buck passing', the station was rebuilt in 1926. The primitive engine shed was also shared and the management functions rotated between the three companies on a four year basis, similar to the Joint arrangement.

Aylesbury therefore became an important station, not only for serving the county town founded on agriculture and engineering, but also for hosting a wide range of railway operations. After Watkin acquired the A&BR, an immediate start was made on upgrading their light single track to double tracks compatible with those of his MS&LR mainline advancing south from Annesley. The route of the A&BR across the Vale of Aylesbury was relatively flat (typically 1 : 200) and would have been fairly straight. Indeed this route had been earlier selected by George Stephenson for his L&BR. Yet the Duke of Buckingham, exerting his power as Chairman of the A&BR, had the line diverted 4 miles west of the 'Pitchcott Gap' to pass nearer his Wotton estate at Quainton. Another example of influence was the construction of a siding to deliver coal to Hartwell House, the home of director John Lee! In the 1930's, a further siding was added to serve an aluminium works on the northern outskirts of Aylesbury, but it was removed after the last war.

Having rebuilt the A&BR, the Met added another station in 1897, Waddesdon Manor, to serve the nearby residence and village of Baron Ferdinand de Rothschild. No doubt his financial eminence influenced this decision, as well as the considerable traffic generated by the estate. He was a frequent user of the Met and sometimes used the two private saloon coaches built by his brother, Lord Alfred, for his own use. These were bought by the Met in 1905, converted into one coach, and used as a spare for the Pullman service that they introduced in 1910.

Only about a mile further on, and 7 miles from Aylesbury, was Quainton Road station, but it could well have been designated a junction as, in effect, three lines met there: 1) the original A&BR route to Verney Junction with the LNWR; 2) the MS&LR from the north, which joined the Met just north of the station in 1898, and 3) the private 6½ mile tramway built in 1871-2 by the Duke of Buckingham and Chandos to serve his house at Wotton and estate as far as Brill. Although the latter did not provide much traffic via Quainton Road, that through Verney Junction and the LNWR was substantial and with the opening of the GCR, and especially their coal trains, the interchange yard was usually packed with wagons.

ooooo000000ooooo

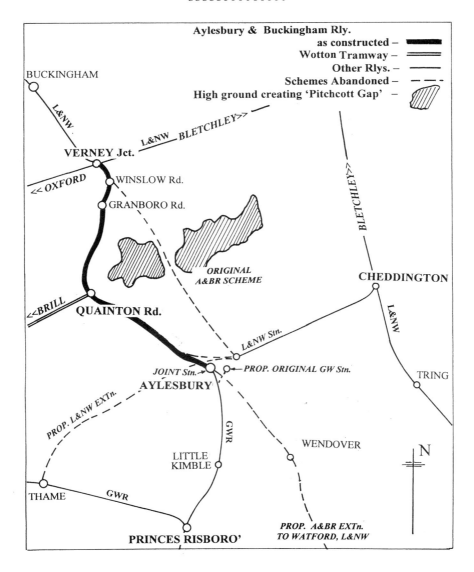

In 1965 and the closing era of steam, an ex-LMS 4-6-0 'Black 5' with an up Nottingham semi-fast train is passing through leafy Bucks towards Great Missenden station near milepost 28½. This marked the boundary of responsibility for maintaining the Joint track, between the GCR to the north and the Met to the south.   *(BCRO)*

The interior of the signal box at Great Missenden with 21 levers. The starting signals were electrically interlocked by the signal box in advance, thus placing control of the train starting with Stoke Mandeville, who were responsible for seeing that the train did not depart before time!   *(BCRO)*

When BR Midland Region took over the Marylebone services in 1958, the Eastern Region took most of the named and express trains with them and by 1960, only a few stopping and semi-fasts were left. Here one headed by another decrepit BR(M) class 5, passes through Great Missenden. Then Neasden shed closed in 1962. *(BCRO)*

Whilst Neasden power station was open, a regular Met working was to collect the necessary coal wagons from Quainton Road. Near Wendover at the crest of the Chilterns, a train of Stephenson & Clarke wagons is hauled by an ex-Met class A 4-4-0T built in 1896.This loco was later preserved and is in the LT Museum. *(H Gordon Tidey)*

The highest point of the Joint was Dutchlands Summit and there, a LT freight train of bricks from Quainton heads for London, behind a K class 2-6-4T loco. This engine was subsequently transferred with most of the Met fleet to the LNER in 1937, who also used it successfully on passenger trains, until it was scrapped in 1943. *(H Gordon Tidey)*

Around 1920, an up GCR suburban train from Aylesbury emerges from underneath Station Road bridge at Wendover. The loco with the slightly domed cab is one of the 9K class 4-4-2 tanks that Robinson designed for this Marylebone service over the Joint. On the right hand side of the bridge is a tall Met signal for better visibility.*(Colin Seabright)*

Around 1956 in BR Eastern Region days, a Gresley class A3 Pacific engine no.60104 'Solario'- from the batch named after famous racing horses - cruises through Wendover with a down express. Wendover station is here in LT hands, - but still with the tall Met signal - and has a tea room on the left.   *(BCRO)*

Also in the mid-1950's, an up mixed goods train, probably diverted from the old GW & GC Joint line due to engineering works, approaches Wendover through a cutting. The engine is an ex-War Department standard 2-8-0 no.90520 designed by Riddles and acquired from the Ministry of Supply at the end of the war.   *(L V Reason)*

During the First War, a 1¾ mile branch line was built north from Wendover station to serve the extensive military camp built on the Rothschild estate at nearby Halton Manor. Its main purpose was to supply the 20,000 troops with fuel. Initially it was steam-operated, but at closure in 1963 it was then being operated by two Fowler 0-4-0 mechanical-diesel locos Here no. AMW 223 is seen on the single track near the canal crossing enroute for Wendover sidings, with an RAF officer in the cab.

(Clive Foxell Collection)

In 1895 the Met built two saloons to carry Lord Alfred Rothschild and his retinue to the City. These were increasingly used for other special occasions and they were rebuilt as a single bogie coach in 1907. It was last used by the Met for the opening of the Stanmore branch and by LT for the 1935 inspection of the Brill branch, which led to its closure.

Originally, the station at Stoke Mandeville was almost as large as the village it served! But in 1926, a few passengers were in evidence for the LNER Aylesbury-bound train from Marylebone. The engine is an ex-Robinson class A5 no.5452 4-6-2 tank, blowing - off after the descent from the Chilterns scarp and now with a clear road. *(R S Carpenter)*

Having decided to push his Met 'Extension' on to Aylesbury rather than Tring, Watkin lost no time in its construction to join the A&BR. This scene captures the ceremony of 'cutting the first sod' for the line at Stoke Road, about a ½ mile south of Aylesbury, in 1891, surrounded by various eminent people as well as several 'hangers on'. *(BCRO)*

After the GWR reluctantly agreed to share their station at Aylesbury with the Met & A&BR, a new one was built on the same site in 1894. Looking north from this new joint station in 1900, one can see beyond the footbridge the original broad gauge goods shed for the GWR branch from Princes Risborough. *(LLRRO/S W A Newton)*

The Met line to Aylesbury opened in 1892 and by 1898, trial trains of the GCR were using the station. However, an acrimonious relationship developed between the parties, culminating in 1904 with a disastrous accident. A GCR class 11B express took the 'S' bend into the station too fast, was de-railed and hit by another train. *(R Sedgewick Coll.)*

It still took until 1906 to sign the formal Agreement creating the 'Joint' and hopefully resolving their differences. But due to the GWR also being involved at Aylesbury, it took another year to start work on improving the track layout that had caused the earlier accident. Here the signal box in the background is about to be moved west. *(S &G Payne)*

The small engine shed, like the rest of Aylesbury, station was shared between the Met, GC and GW - who had the line to Princes Risborough. Around 1916 during the First War, women were recruited to the railways due to the shortage of men. Some took manual jobs and here are cleaning a GCR 8F 4-6-0 no.1095 at Aylesbury. *(CAF Coll.)*

The Met K class 2-6-4T's were assembled by Armstrong-Whitworth to a Met design from modified SECR components, surplus after the first war. This gave a cheap solution to their need for more powerful goods engines, but the size of the K's created clearance problems. Here no.113 is near Aylesbury station with an easy load for Verney Junction.

Another picture of the daily up coal train destined for Neasden power station. Again headed by Met A class no.23, with the fireman contemplating the water column at Aylesbury - complete with a 'fire-devil' to prevent freezing in winter. The bay platform behind holds an LNER train for Marylebone, rather than the usual Met one. *(NRM/LPC)*

The north end of Aylesbury station on a miserable rainy day in 1948. Steam blasts from the safety valve of a LNER 4-6-2 tank engine (ex-GCR Robinson 9N), recently renumbered no.9800 in 1946. The fireman appears to be preparing to pull the water column over to the open top of the side tank. *(Alan J Willmott)*

No.9005, pictured at Aylesbury in 1948, was a post-war replacement for the LNER suburban services. This 2-6-4T design by Thompson - in new shining apple green livery - was part of the LNER modernisation plan to fend off nationalisation. They became the L1 class, but were not liked by the Neasden crews, & existing L1's became L3's. *(Mace)*

Typical of the BR era of the 1950's, a grimy and unidentifiable Gresley V2 class 2-6-2 heads a fast up train through Aylesbury North, bound for Marylebone. On the left is a reminder of the GCR, in the shape of a N5/2 0-6-2T no.69369 (designed by Parker for the MS&LR in 1891), in front of another- but unknown- tank engine. *(L V Reason)*

A scene in the 1950's during the Midland Region era, when the post-war LMS standard engines began to appear on the Joint. With the characteristic backdrop of Aylesbury station and an N5 in the foreground, an Ivatt 4MT 2-6-0 43xx tender loco brings a Met train into the platform, bound for a distant Quainton Road. *(L V Reason)*

A 1950's picture of a Fairburn 2-6-4T at the primitive Aylesbury engine shed. Situated to the west of the 'GWR' platform, it was converted to standard gauge in 1868 and became a sub-shed of Slough. Later it was also used by the Met & GCR under the tripartite arrangements and in BR days became a sub-shed of Neasden. *(British Rail)*

The low sun and the cold of a Christmas Eve in 1962 combine to enhance the exhaust display as the afternoon Marylebone train bound for Nottingham heads out of Aylesbury, past the North signal box. It is headed by the Stanier taper-boiler rebuild of Royal Scot class 4-6-0 no.46112, 'Sherwood Forester'. *(Tony Newman)*

The A&BR was formed in 1861, primarily by the Duke of Buckingham and Sir Harry Verney, who were wealthy enthusiasts for local railway development. Here is a relevant share certificate issued to Sir Harry in 1867. However, it was not until 1868 that it at last obtained access to Aylesbury - by means of the GWR station. *(Donald R Bell)*

The impoverished A&BR could only afford a lightly built single line from Aylesbury to Verney Junction, with a passing loop at Quainton Road (which also facilitated access to the Wotton Tramway). Trains were regulated by the above staffs, the driver only being permitted to move when possessing the one for the relevant section. *(BCRO)*

The impoverished A&BR opened in 1868 by borrowing some lightweight GWR locos compatible with their primitive track. Being standard gauge, they had to be delivered via the LNWR as the GWR tracks to Aylesbury were still of broad gauge. They were of the 517 class of 0-4-2 saddle tanks and until 1870, no.517 above had been no.1040. (LPC)

The view north from Aylesbury station towards Quainton Road in 1897, by when the Met had completed upgrading and doubling the A&BR line. On the right is the original broad gauge goods shed of the GWR branch from Princes Risborough, whilst on the left is the siding for serving Hartwell House (home of an A&BR director). *(S&G Payne)*

As part of the upgrading of the A&BR, in 1897 the Joint built Waddesdon Manor station to serve the large Rothschild estate. It was unusual, in that the main station buildings were on the down platform, unlike the others beyond Harrow. It became Waddesdon in 1922, to avoid confusion with a similar station on the Brill branch.*(GCRS/ Rousselange)*

An early view of Quainton Road station, looking north, after the construction of the junction between the GCR and the Met lines, just visible through the arch of the new bridge. The original signal box can be seen at the base of the signal gantry by the bridge. Passengers could now join the Brill branch to the left of this platform.   *(John Quick)*

A 1947 aerial view of Quainton Road station with the Joint line to Aylesbury to the south *(bottom)* and, to the north, the junction between the GCR mainline and the branch to Verney Junction. The station at the centre of the page shows the Brill branch curving away to the left and then parallel to the road for Waddesdon. *(Crown Copyright 1947)*

MISSING LINK -
QUAINTON TO MORETON PINKNEY

Charles Liddell, a consulting engineer with a world-wide practice and expertise ranging from railways and bridges to submarine telegraph cables, acted as the surveyor for much of the expanding Met line, and it would seem that he was in a relatively privileged position for understanding Watkin's plans. Watkin was notorious for keeping his own counsel, but he had to instruct Liddell on the general objectives to enable the requisite surveys to be undertaken to judge the viability of his various schemes. Indeed, Liddell appears to have gone beyond the strict role of surveying and was trusted not only actively to seek out the likely availability of the relevant land for the routes, but also to negotiate confidentially with the landowners without creating undue rumours that would reach the competitors or raise local opposition. Thus he must have had a reasonable insight into Watkin's Machiavellian schemes and sensibilities.

After the confirmation of the objective of extending the Met line to Aylesbury and absorbing the A&BR, from 1888 Liddell was based in the Vale exploring the possible routes northwards from Verney Junction to join the MS&LR. During this visit he became aware of a proposition to link the Met at Chalfont Road to Moreton Pinkney on the East and West Junction Railway (a line from the MR Bedford - Northampton line via Towcester and Fenny Compton). He negotiated with the proposers and drew it to the attention of Watkin by noting "that this would bring you nearer the MS&LR by some 45 miles at insignificant outlay" and incidentally satisfy his desires for strategic east-west connections to Brackley, Droitwich, Stratford upon Avon and Worcester. Unsurprisingly Watkin was attracted to the scheme but realising that progress depended on completion of the Met to Aylesbury and acquisition of the A&BR; he obtained the agreement to this of the Met Board and the requisite bill was prepared for the 1888-9 session. This then coincided with the consideration of the bill that would authorise the new scheme from Aylesbury to Moreton Pinkney, prepared by the Worcester & Metropolitan Direct Railway (W&MDR), which now also had the backing of Watkin. Indeed, he devolved to Pollitt of the MS&LR the delicate negotiations in order to ensure that it fell in with his broader plans for a north-south route. Remarkably, in spite of Watkin's notorious ability to lobby politicians, the W&MDR bill failed - but ironically in the same session his MS&LR bill to extend their system south from Sheffield to Annesley, under the subterfuge of accessing the Nottingham coalfields, towards the Met at Quainton Road, was successful. When the final link was made it passed about a mile to the west of Moreton Pinkney.

Ironically, the Moreton Pinkney proposal surfaced again later in 1897, but this time from the Met camp, after they had completed upgrading the old A&BR line to Quainton Road. John Bell of the Met was now in open conflict with his erstwhile partner, William Pollitt of the MS&LR, and, sensing that Pollitt would have the upper hand in the completed north-south railway, Bell made a pre-emptive strike by offering to build an extension of the Met some 24 miles northwards to Moreton Pinkney. In this way, the Met contribution to the overall scheme would be enhanced - and with it Bell's position! Nevertheless, Pollitt saw through the ploy and that it would give Bell even further excuses for prevarication, so he imposed unacceptable conditions on any agreement which effectively defeated the proposal.

oooooOOOOooooo

The proposed Met Extension to Moreton Pinkney with the junction at Quainton Road, from the plans prepared by Charles Liddell for the 1890 session of Parliament.

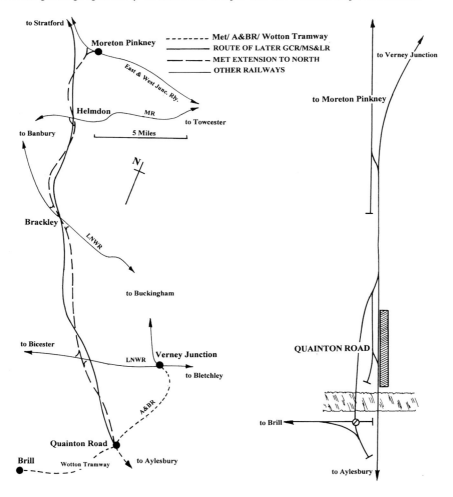

QUAINTON TO BRILL & VERNEY JUNCTION

The 3rd Duke of Buckingham & Chandos was not only forward-looking in improving his estate by adding indigenous industries, such as a brick works, to supply the neighbourhood but also took a paternalistic attitude to his workers. So the operation of these local industries and the building of his tramway were phased to provide work during the winter when little agricultural work could be done. Being on private land, no legislation was necessary and although it was initially horse-drawn, crude steam locomotives were introduced and soon a rudimentary passenger service was operating as the Wotton Tramway. This relative success reawakened the ambitions of the Duke and Sir Harry Verney, who in 1883 promoted extending the tramway by 12 miles west to Oxford as the Oxford, Aylesbury and Metropolitan Junction Railway. This title reveals the link with Watkin who, seeing the prospect of the Met reaching Oxford, quickly became a director. However the death of the Duke in 1889 delayed matters and it was 1894 before his estate leased the tramway to a new company: the Oxford & Aylesbury Tramroad. They improved the primitive line and stock to some extent but were overtaken by events - again in the shape of Watkin.

As part of the legislation for extending the Met to Aylesbury, Watkin obtained authorisation to buy the A&BR and upgraded the line with the first through services to Baker Street, starting in 1897. The original station at Quainton was to the north of the present one and, with the Brill branch approaching from the west, the connection via a turntable was replaced by curving their line south alongside the new mainline platform to join the down line. Leaving for Brill, the single line branch ran beside the road to a station at Waddesdon Road, the first rail link with Waddesdon Manor, with a typical minimalist timber platform for one coach. Then downhill to Westcott, which once boasted a stationmaster, and under the later GC mainline (which bypassed the Joint in 1906) to Wotton station. The line then climbed some 130 ft to Brill about 2¾ miles further, first passing Church Siding on the right - which meandered down to a coal wharf at Kingswood where a horse was used to fly-shunt any wagons. It then travelled on to the timber platform and hut that constituted Wood Siding, located at a clearing in the middle of Grenville's Wood. Crossing the GWR mainline to Birmingham (which also formed part of the GW & GC arrangements) and, past on the right a small siding to a brick works, a gradient of 1 in 44 brought one to Brill station - but still almost a mile from the town and some 250 ft below!

In later years the branch was operated by a venerable Met A class loco and Ashbury coach. The highlight of their schedule was the daily school train which left Brill at 07.57 arriving at Quainton Road at 08.30, where the children had to de-train for 12 min whilst the train gained the main line, and then proceeded to Aylesbury for 08.55! Although the Met publicised Brill as "the favourite hunting seat of Edward the Confessor", traffic on the branch never expanded significantly and with the take over in 1933 of the Met by LT (with their lack of enthusiasm for steam operation), the days of this marginal line were numbered. The Joint terminated its tenancy in 1935 and sold their assets, with the freehold reverting to Earl Temple.

The original Met mainline to Verney Junction was joined by the new GC mainline at Upper South Farm Junction about 1/3 mile to the north of Quainton Rd. Bearing to the right the Met double track had to climb Hogshaw Bank at about 1 in 115 and then downhill to reach Granborough/ Grandborough Road station. It continued downhill at 1 in 250 to Winslow Road station: both stations originally had manually operated level crossings and were similar to Quainton, being of like design and distance from their implied locations! As the line approached the Oxford - Bletchley LNWR line, it swung back to the west to enter Verney Junction past the Met interchange yard into one face of the island platform. Banbury/Oxford trains used the other face and Bletchley services a single platform. Being in splendid isolation, it was only a junction with little local traffic from the public house and the few surrounding houses. Sadly this 'Ultima Thule' of the Met never lived up to the hopes of those two railway enthusiasts, the Duke of Buckingham and his friend Sir Harry Verney, or even Sir Edward Watkin, who had envisaged it as a potential 'Clapham Junction' of the Vale of Aylesbury.

For similar reasons to the run-down of the Brill branch, the Joint (when under LPTB and LNER) closed their Verney Junction branch to passengers in 1936 and had the line singled by 1940. However, during the war, with the construction of a link at Calvert between the LNWR and the GCR lines, it proved to be part of a useful relief line around London. Nevertheless after the end of the war the goods service was withdrawn in 1947 and the track lifted in 1957. Eventually, after BR Midland Region took responsibility for the Marylebone line, all regular passenger services north of Aylesbury were withdrawn from September 1966.

However, with the resurgence under Chiltern Railways this abandoned route may soon awake from its slumbers.

ooooo000ooooo

After the 1923 'grouping', the LNER provided the Aylesbury - Verney Junction 'shuttle' service consisting of a tank engine plus auto coach. Latterly, the loco was usually an ex-GER class F7 2-4-2 tank no.8307, here seen in the mid 1930's at a deserted Quainton Road station with an up train bound for Aylesbury. *(NRM/Rhodes)*

Around 1900, the Brill train is at Quainton Road station alongside the new platform face built by the Met to accommodate the branch from the west. Although now formally part of the Met, they had found it necessary to retain the venerable, but lightweight, stock in view of the fragile track. The loco was Manning-Wardle 0-6-0ST 'Huddersfield'. *(LTM)*

The Met subsequently re-laid the Brill branch track to a higher standard and enhanced some primitive stations. This charming vignette of the 1920's shows Wotton 'station' in a timeless sylvan setting. In the background towards Quainton is the bridge carrying the GC line to the GW & GC joint line, built to outflank the then obstructive Met.   *(LTM)*

The next minimal station along the branch towards Brill was Wood Siding, which was virtually over the GWR mainline. The posters advertise how to get to the convenient fleshpots of London and the North, whilst the ladder that can just be seen in the background was said to have been used to lookout for the next approaching train!

With better track, the lighter engines of the Met could now work the Brill branch. First the D class and then the old A class 4-4-0 tank locos had this duty and here in 1930, one is taking water at Brill's dilapidated shed and forge. Nos.41 and 23 took it in turns to work the line for a week before returning to Neasden with a goods train.   *(H Casserley)*

A Joint goods train leaves Quainton Road to branch off from the mainline to Verney Junction. Appropriately, it is hauled by 'Brill', an ex-Met G class 0-6-4T engine, that was acquired with most of the Met steam locos by the LNER in 1937. It has become an M2 class no.6157, the first of the class that was withdrawn in 1943.   *(S H Freese)*

101

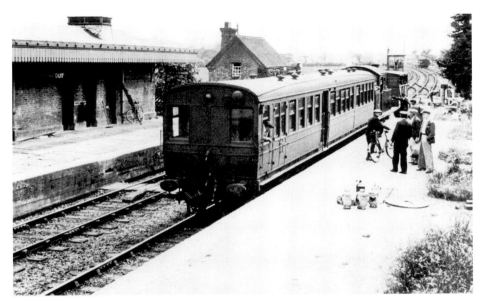

At the time of the imminent closure to passengers of the branch to Verney Junction in 1936, the up 'shuttle' pauses at Granborough Road station. The driver in the autocoach looks back at his fireman with a class F7 no.8307, which is hauling a cattle wagon. In the background, is the level crossing and the keeper's cottage. *(LTM)*

A quiet day at Winslow Road station in the early 1930's, looking from the level crossing towards Aylesbury. The Met added the footbridge, which obscured the signal and the signal box in the right foreground. Following closure for passenger traffic in 1936, the tracks were singled in 1937 and the LNE main line junction at Quainton eased.*(L&GRP)*

The furthest and bleakest point on the Joint lay some 50 miles from London at Verney Junction, created by the optimists of the A&BR in 1868, with a name reflecting the influence of the local Verney family. This early picture shows the new platforms and ticket office, built when the A&BR was acquired by the Met in 1892.(*Clive Foxell Coll.*)

A later view of about 1914 shows the centre of Verney Junction station with the LNWR Oxford-Bletchley and the Buckingham lines platforms to the right. On the left is the Met platform with a Baker Street ('main line') train, comprising an E class 0-4-4T no.82, with Ashbury coaches and Pullman car, ready to depart on the 2 hr journey.   *(LPC)*

A 1946 aerial view of Verney Junction (with the west to the top of the page) confirms its splendid isolation. The LMSR Oxford-Bletchley line runs from top to bottom, whilst their route to Buckingham branches off to the right. The Joint line from Quainton Road curves round through 90° to approach the station from bottom left.*(Crown Copyright 1946)*

PEOPLE OF THE JOINT

Ticket Office Clerk's Tale - Iris Prior

As a girl before the last war, Iris lived with her parents at Willesden. A friend of her parents knew a young man, Charles Prior, who had started in 1926 as a cleaner at the LNER loco sheds at Colwick near Nottingham. Now, as a fireman had been posted to Neasden shed, but was sleeping in the mess as he lacked suitable accommodation. The mutual friend successfully begged them to take him in but for some time Iris took little notice of Charles, until he was transferred to Woodford Halse and yet still returned to their house at the weekends. They started going out together and with their engagement, Charles applied for a transfer back to Neasden - but instead was sent to Chesham, a place unknown to both of them!

Matters were accelerated by Iris's house being bombed in 1940 so their wedding was hastily moved to Nottingham, after which they found 'digs' (two rooms) in Chesham, which enabled Charles to be near the 'shuttle' he operated, Iris to commute to work in London and her mother to join them. Iris's journey took a wearing 3½ hours daily and,as a result of a chance encounter with Mr Taylor, the station master of Chesham, she was offered a job in the booking office. It being wartime, she had to seek release at the Labour Office from her existing job at British-Thompson-Houston and then go to Baker Street for a thorough LT medical examination and tests in English and mathematics. Passing these meant that now Iris of the Met and Charles of the GCR would be working together on the Joint - albeit on different shifts!

Life in the booking office at Chesham began at 5.15am for the first shift which lasted until 1.15pm. On the first morning Iris walked there in the virtually total darkness of the blackout, to be instructed on how to issue tickets and 'cash up', before being left on her own to deal with passengers who were arriving in large numbers to catch the early trains. Sometimes the queue stretched as far as the brewery at White Hill, because a number of small City traders had moved home to Chesham in order to avoid the bombing, and travelled back to their businesses each day - often with suitcases full of their more precious stock. Iris easily recalls the return fares of 1/5½d to Baker Street and 1/6½d to Aldgate for the last workmen's tickets on the 7.30am! At this time the 'shuttle' was crowded to capacity, but as the peak passed there were enquiries to be answered for the times of trains and tickets anywhere in the UK. First class tickets had been withdrawn at the outbreak of the war but were re-introduced on the Aylesbury and other mainline services after a few months. Then at 10am, the astute Chief Clerk would arrive to check that all was well and Iris would take yesterday's ticket money down to the bank - unescorted and with the pound notes stuffed down her trousers!

Meanwhile, her colleague Marion,with the porter and his boy assistant, were dealing with the large numbers of parcels handled by Chesham. In those days, most of the Post Office and newspaper deliveries came through the station. Also, apart from the local specialities of baskets of watercress and mushrooms (when in season), each day there were also domestic and commercial parcels, for example Van Houten daily sent a parcel of chocolate and cocoa, to every Woolworths in the country. Most of the material for the US Air Force at Bovingdon also came through Chesham. Even coffins (with bodies) were dealt with by the parcels team!

On Friday, the 11am train brought the week's wages in a big leather bag. Iris had to divide them up into the traditional paper coin bags and distribute amongst the staff. The remainder of the shift and the following afternoon spell were relatively quiet, although there was always something going on: messages from Mr Butterfield the signalman about the running of the trains - the stationmaster calling in to warm himself by the fine fire that was kept going in the ticket office and Mr Hobbs of the goods office to discuss the ever increasing amount of wartime goods traffic, and to have a cup of tea. One day, Iris turned to the ticket office window to find a gentleman asking to be directed to the police station so that he could report, under wartime regulations, as a foreigner in the town. Seeing he was carrying a heavy bag, Iris offered to keep it for him until he returned, but shortly afterwards a passer-by rushed in to say this man had collapsed outside. Iris dashed out and found that he was dead, and looking for someone to help turned to a young man in the waiting room. He hurried to the body only to find that it was his father.

With the blackout the last shift was the most difficult, with large numbers of people returning from London and a surprising number going there and then the inevitable rush of the last trains. Those arriving on the last trains, which included many servicemen, often either had no tickets or scraps of paper purporting to be tickets and being alone Iris had to judge when to shut a blind eye. To get away as soon as possible after the last train which arrived at 1.15am involved another rush to close the ticket sales and account for the day's sales - or 'cash up' as it was known. Sales were reckoned by looking at the change in the number on each stack of the Edmonson tickets and with experience, a good estimate could be made of the final figures. These had to match the money taken for the day and creative accounting was sometimes employed to achieve the desired result! After locking-up, Iris made her way home again along the Backs in total darkness, but later she found that the local policeman, George Hearn, had kept a look-out for her.

Iris had a very happy time at the ticket office, but when the war ended, the servicemen began returning to their old jobs and her pregnancy made it an opportune time to leave. Her husband, Charlie, returned to work from Neasden depot as a driver, working the turns to Nottingham and Sheffield, then in 1956 he left driving to take extra responsibility at the supervisory grade, overseeing the drivers and stock operating out of Marylebone. With the advent of dieselisation in 1960, he opted for retirement.

The Engineman's Tale - Ken Palmer

Charlie's job on the 'shuttle' was taken by Ken Palmer, who had joined the LT in 1947 as a stationman/shunter at Northwood, before moving to the LNER engine shed at Neasden as a cleaner and soon passing as a fireman in 1948. He then transferred to the 'shuttle' that oscillated between Chalfont & Latimer on the main line and Chesham. *There was a certain irony in this because since 1931, Ken's family have farmed the land along the Vale at Chesham that Watkin bought for his abortive extension from Chesham to Tring.* Until 1940, this train retained the old Met formation of an E class 0-4-4T plus Dreadnought coaches, which involved the loco running round the train at each end of the trip, and at Chalfont & Latimer this necessitated drawing the train out of the platform. With the outbreak of war, the drawback of this time consuming operation led to replacement of the 'shuttle' by LNER class C13's (ex-GCR 9K 4-4-2 tank engines) fitted with vacuum-operated control gear, which enabled the train to be driven from either end. The replacement coaches were old Ashbury stock of 1899, which had been later converted into electric multiple sets, and were then held in the strategic war reserve. Their conversion back to steam-working left a driver's position at the end of the leading/trailing coach, although in practice either the fireman or driver took turns to drive with the regulator/brake in the front coach. This was marshalled so that the engine pulled the train over the sharp reverse bends from Chesham and then up the 1 in 66 out of the Chess valley for it's 3½ mile run. The engine usually faced Chalfont so that, when working hard up the gradient, the crown of the boiler would remain covered with water.

The locomotive crew of the 'shuttle' worked a basic three-shift rota of 8 hours, but there was an additional shift that involved shovelling 10 tons of coal from a wagon onto the primitive wooden coaling stage. His colleagues included Ted Copperthwaite and Sid Herbert (chargehand). The night-shift of 10.25pm to 6.25am returned to Chesham with the last train of weary passengers at 1.10am and after a check that the train was empty, the coaches were shunted into a siding. Carriage doors were locked in order to try and prevent passing 'diddycoys' from bedding down for the night. Next, a load of 10 or 11 goods wagons were taken up to the sidings at Chalfont & Latimer, afterwards the engine returned with a similar

The interior of Chesham ticket office remained virtually unchanged from this scene of 1908 until Iris Prior arrived in 1940. This early view, with James Woodward (left) and 'Tug' Wilson surrounded by Edmonson card tickets, reflects the recent formation of the Joint, with a Great Central poster just visible through the hatch.   *(Jean Podbury)*

During Iris's time at Chesham station, it still handled most of the Post Office mail by train. This late 1930's LT era picture shows a Met fast 'through' train being unloaded by a local postman. The engine is no.97 and named 'Brill', a member of the 0-6-4T G class and soon to be transferred to the LNER.   *(Clive Foxell Coll.)*

The evening sunlight casts shadows over the classic scene of the engine of the Chesham 'shuttle' about to take water from the column in Chesham station during 1951. The engine is an ex-GCR class 9K, built by J. G. Robinson in 1904 specifically to handle their expanding London commuter traffic. Much later, as an LNER C13 no. 7416, this one returned to the Chesham branch in 1941 to operate the new 'push-pull' service to Chalfont & Latimer. *(L V Reason)*

Later in July 1955, the same engine, BR no.67416, and Ashbury coaches are again captured simmering gently in Chesham station, but by now the aborted pre-war plans for electrification of the branch have been re-activated. Behind in the extensive goods yard the daily pick-up goods waits to remove some empty coal wagons. *(H C Casserley)*

The background with Chalfont & Latimer still being developed, the original station awnings and a 'shuttle' comprising a Met E class 0-4-4T with the better Dreadnought coaches suggests the early 1930's. Equally, the suspicious group of boys with caps and badges are reminiscent of 'Just William' and his Gang! *(NMR/Rokeby Coll.)*

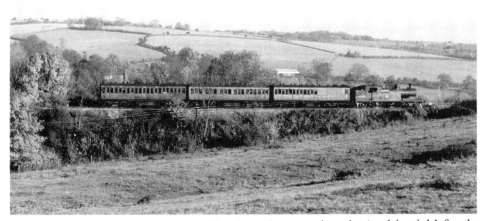

In 1959, work is starting on the electrification scheme and so the 'end is nigh' for the steam Chesham 'shuttle'. This shows C13 class 4-4-2T no.67416 with the vintage Ashbury ex-electric stock - storming up the 1 in 66 gradient in typical style, out of the Chess Valley near Quill Hall, towards Chalfont & Latimer. *(L V Reason)*

load to Chesham, where the wagons were shunted and placed in precisely the position required by the local traders to unload. Any subsequent movement would be charged to them! The opportunity was then taken to replenish the oil, water and coal levels of the engine, but the facilities at Chesham were primitive, with an ancient wooden coaling stage which had to be stocked by shovelling the coal from wagons and then up again into the bunker of the engine. The coal came from the Yorkshire coalfields and was well-suited to the ex-GCR locos, but as shortages worsened, an occasional wagon of Welsh anthracite had to be used with dire effects as it quickly burnt through. Water also presented problems due to the chalky nature of the local water, and although water treatment blocks were regularly added to the tanks, from time to time the fireman had to scrape the scale out of the injectors by hand. Some of the water supplies came from local streams and this probably accounted for the fish - who did not seem to mind the warm water - sometimes found in the loco tanks!

During the long night-shift, there was often the opportunity for the crew to have a surreptitious sleep on 'the cushions' in the warm Ashbury coaches before the next event of the arrival of the early morning newspaper train from Marylebone at 5.00 am. This train was the last vestige of the services originating with the creation of the Joint in 1906 and ended up operated by a DMU in 1967. Although not in the public timetable, a few people who worked on the morning newspapers returned home on this train and other knowing passengers used it as an early train up to London leaving Chesham 5.40am. Around this time two policemen usually paid the first call of the day to check that all was well.

The first 'shuttle' ran at 6.25 but the day shift began earlier at 6.00am. In winter this could be grim due to the tendency for snow to drift across the exposed track as it climbed up and out of the Chess valley to Raans Farm at an altitude of 400ft. In such bad weather, LT ran a steam engine and four wagons to and fro on the branch at night in order to keep the line open and Ken well remembers driving through a virtual white tunnel in which he could lean out of the cab and take a handful of snow. Only in the 1960's were fences erected to reduce this drifting problem. Fog could also be a big problem when signals became invisible and the crews had to rely on fogmen posted at signals and huddled over a small fire with their warning detonators at the ready, or climb the ladder themselves to be able to see the aspect shown by the signal arm.

Further breaks were taken whilst the two 'through' trains ran in the morning and evening and the opportunity was taken to shunt the day's wagons into the order requested by Mr Darvell in the goods office for the daily 'pick-up' goods train that called at most stations to Quainton Road.

The second day-shift started at 2.25pm and was largely routine. Mid-week, the engine would be returned to Neasden shed for a boiler wash-out and servicing. This involved running the 'shuttle' up to Chalfont & Latimer with an engine at both ends of the train. Ken remembers that a similar formation was employed when the only C13's available for the Chesham 'shuttle' were not fitted for auto working - thus two crews and a guard sometimes out-numbered the passengers! On a Sunday, the coaches were taken to Rickmansworth and then by a Met electric loco to Neasden LT works, to be left for cleaning and exchanged with the spare three-coach set. This manoeuvre is described by Croome, see p135 for reference.

During 1936, in order to replace what LT saw as the anachronistic steam operated 'shuttle', they had borrowed one of the new GWR diesel railcars (built by AEC) for use on the branch. The results encouraged an LT Acton study of a larger vehicle but this was abandoned due to the war. Later as the C13/Ashbury sets grew older, in 1956 LT again tried a diesel railcar. This time, one of the new lightweight ACV 4-wheel cars of bus-like construction that BR were trialing as a replacement for their steam operated branches. Ken and his driver kept a C13 in steam by the Chesham coaling stage as a standby and, although it was not needed, the noise of the wheels screeching as it negotiated the curves at Waterside could be heard all over Chesham. Ted Copperthwaite, who had been trained to drive it, was not impressed and reported that metal filings from the wheels could be found beside the track at these tight spots!

When the pre-war plans for electrification were revived and the veteran C13 tank engines were scrapped in 1960, Ken transferred back to Neasden BR shed driving local trains. Next as steam was phased out, there was a spell of bringing coal trains from Aylesbury on to Neasden power station which supplied the Met and then Ken went back to Neasden on diesel shunting duties. This inevitably led to becoming a driver on the new BR multiple diesel fleet that were taking over all services from Aylesbury. Thus he retired in 1989 after some 42 years service on the Joint and at home today looks out over the route that Watkin planned to Tring.

The Signalman's Tale - Tony ('Bob') Geary
Tony is a member of a long-standing railway family: Bob, his grandfather, worked for Firbank the contractor in the 1880's on the construction of the Met 'extension' and stayed on to become head permanent way ganger on the Chesham branch. Bob's son, also a Robert, joined the Joint at Chesham in 1906 as a parcels boy and later became a driver of the A class tank engines that then operated the Chesham branch. At that time, they had to run round the coaches at each end of the branch and fit in some shunting of wagons between trips.

When LT absorbed the Met in 1933, Bob took the 'juice' and became a motorman based at Neasden shed. The family moved into a house on the adjacent 'Neasden Village' that had been built by Watkin (in a brief instance of paternalism) during the 1880's for his employees, in what was then open country. Their son, Tony, well remembers living in Aylesbury Street (near Chesham St., Quainton St. and Verney St.), together with the Met-built shops, school and church. He also recalls the names of Met neighbours such as Ling (power station), Clacker (guard), Gerkin and Kettle (signalmen), Bond, Emery & Quacker (Inspectors), Herbert - Sid, later of the Chesham shuttle, Honour & Johnson (drivers), Coggins (p.way), Honey (ticket collector) and Hunt (shunter). Whilst the 'Village' was now being engulfed by the advancing suburbs of London, the main concern of his mother was the dirt that fell from the nearby large Met generating station, built in 1903 to supply the power for the Met electrification to Harrow. The boilers were supplied almost every day by a Met hauled train from Quainton Road of Stephenson & Clarke coal wagons from their north Yorkshire mines. The Neasden scene was dominated by the tall wooden-shuttered cooling towers of the power station until demolished in 1968, when suddenly most of the houses on the Met estate featured new wooden fences and sheds!

Tony himself joined the railways (albeit the GWR!) at the age of 14 years as a parcels boy at Westbourne Park, before soon finding his forte with LT at the signal box at Wood Lane. Now he had to respond to the call of 'bobby' which originated from the use of policemen to control movements on the early railways. In his new post, the young Tony was surprised how much of the job he was expected to do whilst the proper signalman tended his nearby allotment. A particular feature of Wood Lane station was a moving platform controlled from the box: operated by compressed air this enabled the platform clearance to be changed in a very restricted site. In 1945 he went to Wembley Park (95 levers and 25 bellcodes) and then Acton Town (125 levers), where he disliked working the 'split shifts' which did not allow him enough time to get home between the turns in different signal boxes.

Then to Baker Street (18 levers), still as the box boy, where his first duties were to prepare the booking sheets for the next day. This took about 3 hours and subsequently on these he would have to record scrupulously all traffic movements and orders relevant to the box. Working a three-shift roster, he also took all the phone calls. As there were no train describers at that time, all messages were received on 11 telephones around the box - running from one to another, this turned out to be a frantic job! For an extra 2/6d per week he also worked the platform indicators which were controlled by a 4ft long stud-contact drum with codes for the various destinations. In addition, he had to quickly nip down the stairs to check the headcodes of incoming trains or pass hot water to the drivers for their tea caddies. Apart from the usual trains, he remembers the weekly special for the surrounding Chiltern Court buildings. This usually consisted of a Met Bo-Bo electric loco hauling wagons of coal for heating the prestige flats and - having unloaded, removing their rubbish. Access was achieved via a siding off no.1 platform operated by a massive 2ft long key kept in the signal box, for the manual ground frame,. The movement of this train required the assistance of another Bo-Bo loco on layover for the complex shunting necessary to enable the train to return to Neasden.

Tony's shift often started at 7am with getting the breakfast for the signalmen which involved taking rationbooks to the local shop for the food, including the essential condensed milk for their tea. After cooking their breakfast on the minuscule stove in the corner of the box he had to take over operating the levers, booking and telephones while they ate! Then at 8.15am Mr Barker, the Divisional Inspector, arrived and, amidst much banter and snuff-taking with the signalman, would operate the levers for about 45 minutes. Next the stationmaster would come at about 9 am to give the signalman another meal break, but Tony was still working the box!

At that time women recruited during the war were still employed in the signalboxes and, although Tony had in practice been acting as a signalman for some time, he could not be considered for such a post until he was over 20 years old. So he was moved to an LT-Southern joint box at Surrey Docks Junction on a salubrious site over a mile from the station, next to a canal and without a toilet or water, which was delivered by train or by a bucket from the canal. In 1951 he moved to another joint box, this time at Ealing Broadway (31 manual levers), controlling the interchange with the BR(W) plus the electric levers ('punches') for the Central line.

Promoted to signalman in 1955, at Wembley Park he was involved in the changeover from the original signal box, via a temporary box on the platform, to the present box with an electric console, which needed 5 men to operate it rather than the original 2. It was a busy job with 25 different bell codes, but well-ordered even during the pressure of events at Wembley, which involved several specials stabled in Wembley Park sheds. These were usually 1920 'F' stock with elliptical end windows and manual doors - known as 'Tanks' because they were somewhat overpowered. On one such occasion, the waiting driver failed to observe the green signal and remained in the sheds, but not to be outwitted, the signalmen booked the phantom train through to Baker Street and back again! Another odd event occurred when a normal service train, full of passengers, was accidentally diverted

The three generations of the Geary family that have worked on the Joint. From the left: most recently, Tony a signalman; his father Robert, shown here as a station boy at Chesham and who became an engine driver; his grandfather Bob, who helped to build the Met and stayed on as a p.w. ganger. *(Tony Geary & Maurice Sawyer)*

The interior of Amersham signal box in the 1950's with the track diagram still showing the station name as 'Amersham & Chesham Bois', which was only used between 1922 - 1939! The weight of the early Met signal arms caused problems and to counterbalance them cast-iron spectacle plates were used at Amersham, lasting until 1961.*(Tony Geary)*

The standard Met designed signal box of 1889 at Chesham (20 levers and 4 spares) in the drab post-war LT colours of grey and cream. Following the 1961 electrification it was finally taken out of service in 1966 and is now preserved. (*Tony Geary*)

The 'leaning signal box of Rickmansworth', under construction in 1961 as part of the LT electrification scheme to Amersham and Chesham. Built behind the Met down starter signal, unfortunately the foundations allowed one side of the building to subside, giving the floor a distinct slope! (*Geoff Gamble Coll*)

through Neasden sheds and out at the other end, causing a bewildered passenger to write to the local paper. Another strange event he witnessed from the box involved the nightmare of a suicide attempt. He saw a man on the platform throw himself in front of an oncoming Bakerloo train but, although it was too late for Tony to do anything about it, the train, being only a 4-car set, pulled up at its rightful place - some distance short of where the man stood on the tracks - he then ran off out of the station.

1960 saw Tony move to Harrow on the Hill station where the Joint traditions died hard. The stationmaster was very conscious of the complex arrangements of the past and Tony was only the second LT signalman to work in this box, being referred to as a 'Boardsman' with any conversation passed via the signalboy. It took some 8 weeks to be 'passed' for the Harrow box including spells at both the 'London' and 'country' ends. At that time the yard was busy with a permanent shunting engine and dealing with about 3 Marylebone goods trains each day and the South Harrow gas works trip, which involved a signalman accompanying the train to set the manual points at the works. At that time a crane, which was the only piece of Joint rolling stock, was still in a siding at Harrow. Perhaps it was left here because of the number of derailments at manual points in the yard. Particular attention had to be given to workings with BR steam locomotives as these were not fitted with the fail-safe signalling tripcocks used on LT (and later Chiltern Railways) stock. He was also present during the notorious incident when the up 'South Yorkshireman' arrived at the wrong platform at Harrow and, being unable to move forward to the Marylebone line, was diverted into the goods yard and, with some shunting, regained platform 5 for Marylebone.

However, the grading system changed, introducing a new level of 'Traffic Regulator', from which Tony at Harrow was barred under an earlier 1942 Joint agreement, and the post went to a BR(E) signalman. Therefore, Tony opted to become a Relief Signalman for most of the Met Extension, which needed familiarity with all the line to Aylesbury before being tested and passed out by the District Inspector. Life was hard, working a 3-shift system with 7 days 'on' and 1 day 'off' in 21.

At this time snow and particularly fog were ever present dangers in winter and previous incidents were still well-remembered, such as the collision in 1945 when Bo-Bo electric loco no.19 with the 08.36 Baker Street-Aylesbury train in dense fog ran into the back of the 08.10 Aldgate-Watford train standing at Northwood home signal. The debris was then hit by another train, killing three people. The investigation concluded that the speed of no.19 was excessive, having regard to the visibility.

Being high above Harrow station it was often difficult to judge the visibility at track level so special 'fog posts' were erected to help the signalmen to judge the conditions. In addition, a fog watch was instituted with a man on the platform to watch out for the tail lights of the trains. Fogs seemed worse in those days and on some occasions Tony and his colleagues were themselves trapped on trains and unable to get to work.

Rickmansworth box was originally at the south end of the down platform, but in 1961 it was rebuilt in brick LT style at the north end. This was on a steep embankment and before long the box began to subside. Soon Tony noticed that anything dropped on the floor would roll to the front of the box and the guttering at the rear of the roof proved useless. However, LT stabilised the building and the gutter was transferred to the front! LT was now committed to the electrification to Amersham and the name boards that were laboriously slotted into a post on each platform to mark the destination of the next train (not always accurately) were removed. But the signalmen took understandable pride in the slick changeover between steam and electric traction and sometimes, to speed matters up, they would run back the incoming down Met Bo-Bo electric loco behind a southbound train. However, some unusual workings presented problems, as the signal box changes were set by a programme controller and any manual override had to be done at a suitable blank part of the programme scroll. Indeed for some movements such as for the Watford Tip over the north curve, the whole scroll had to be taken out! Even at this time the declining number of BR steam trains for the north, that did not stop at Rickmansworth, still tried to exceed the speed restriction through the station in order to help climb the gradient to Amersham. By 1962 Tony moved to Chesham, Amersham and Chorley Wood boxes, and at the latter he remembers that an ex-Marylebone train reversed there each weekday.

Work was now well under way on the long delayed electrification from Harrow to Amersham and Chesham, involving the replacement of several bridges - with provision for improved roads, notably near Northwood - platform extensions, substations, modified track layouts and simplified signalling. At the start of the new services in 1961, they were operated by the existing Met multiple-electric T stock and Bo-Bo electric locomotives until deliveries of the new LT 'aluminium' A60 sets were complete in 1962. Then going to Chesham - Tony found long-serving colleagues operating this archetypal outpost of the Joint in a manner virtually unchanged for many years. As part of the electrification programme, a short-lived bay platform had been added in anticipation of increasing the frequency of the single line branch service, but this came to naught and the extra track was soon removed. Although the Shuttle dominated the day, morning and evening were enlivened by fast through 'city' trains, the early morning with a

DMU bringing the newspapers from Marylebone and the afternoon still by a steam hauled pick-up goods.

Then in 1964,Tony had a spell at Farringdon box where confusion still reigned over the use of old Met, Midland and GNR bellcodes. A further period at Harrow followed where there was a resurgence of steam, due to the use of Marylebone for trains diverted as a result of the rebuilding of Euston, and various overnight trains and specials. However, he witnessed the growing dominance of the DMU's in the overall rundown by BR(M), culminating in the closure of the line beyond Aylesbury in September 1966. During those rather sad final days of steam on the Joint, a consolation was the appearance of a tremendous variety of steam power with a prevalence of dilapidated B1's and then class 5's limping through. Tony then had a period of relief working all along the Met, during which he became increasingly frustrated with the pressures, before returning in 1978 to a permanent post at Harrow and finally retiring in 1987, after 44 years' service. However, he still tends his allotment close beside the Chesham branch line - on ground originally bought by Sir Edward Watkin and only recently sold by LUL.

The Tale of Fred France - Driver of the 'Sheffield Special'

Fred joined the MS&LR at Gorton and became a passed fireman in time to be on the engine which hauled the first public GCR train out of Marylebone in 1899. Subsequently moving to Neasden shed around 1902, he progressed up the grades so that by 1914 he had become a driver on the spare 'Director' GC class 11 4-4-0 duty. Often this was no.437, 'Charles Stuart-Wortley'. In 1918 he had risen to the no.2 link and by 1921, was often in charge of the fast 'piped goods' with either nos. 460 or 461, new Robinson 4-cylinder 4-6-0's. Then he was promoted to the top link at Neasden, often dealing with the 'Newspaper Flyer' which left Marylebone precisely at 2.32am with a most demanding schedule timed to reach Sheffield at 6.25am. However, the more well-known crack GCR express train over the Met & GC Joint line was the celebrated the 3.15 pm 'Sheffield Special', scheduled non-stop at speed over the 164.7 miles from Marylebone.

Perhaps one other reason it was 'special' could be that it initially carried few passengers in up to five coaches - of which one was usually slipped at Leicester. From the locomotive aspect, in the early years of the Joint, it was almost a holiday outing for the powerful Robinson Atlantics. A Mr Bell recorded one such run with the basic 5 coaches (albeit all of the heavy Robinson clerestory design) behind a 4-4-2 engine No.1091. As far as Leicester, where one coach was dropped, the load must have been around 180-190 tons.

An aggressive start was made from Marylebone so that Harrow was reached in 12min 58sec, over a minute early, at an average speed of 44.5mph. With a clear path on entering the Joint, Rickmansworth was passed after 21min 4sec, having reached 60mph. However the climb up the Chilterns to Amersham inevitably reduced the speed to some 39.8mph, but after breasting Dutchlands Summit, the downhill run into the next stop at Aylesbury produced 67.3mph, until slowing for the approach curve into the station gave an arrival of some 31secs under the scheduled 45mins for the 38 miles from Marylebone. Now in the Vale of Aylesbury, Quainton Road was passed 2mins before the scheduled 53mins and the Atlantic easily maintained a speed of 60-66 mph to Woodford, resulting in running some 2mins ahead of time. This performance was sustained to Leicester, arriving 1min 8sec before the tabled 109min for the 103.1 miles. However, on this occasion, the completion of the journey was spoilt by a signal delay of about 2min outside Nottingham which meant that the arrival at Sheffield (164.7 miles) was just 18 sec over the scheduled 177min.

Later in 1936, O S Nock was travelling on the Joint, at a time when the new LNER 'Sandringhams' were beginning to replace the ex-GC 'Directors' on the crack trains. Here, with due acknowledgements, are his notes of one such journey on the 4.55pm down express behind 4-4-0 No. 5504 *Jutland,* which showed that the Robinson engines had lost none of their capabilties. "As we started away from Marylebone on this trip, with 295 tons behind the tender, my thoughts went back to the earliest days of the 'Directors', when the famous 3.15pm 'Sheffield Special' had a load of no more than five bogie coaches.

Driver Fred France of Neasden was another of those splendid enginemen, steeped in Great Central tradition for hard and punctual running, and from the outset he put No.5504 to her task with a vigour that was exhilarating to hear from the train. The Aylesbury route, with its sharp gradients, is a very awkward proposition with anything approaching a heavy train, but we dashed out to Rickmansworth in a faster time than one often records over the first 17¼ miles with crack trains out of Paddington or Waterloo, on level roads; 30½ mph at Kilburn; 66½ at Neasden – some acceleration!; 65½ at Pinner; 56 over Northwood summit, and then easily down to Watford Junction in preparation for the very bad slack through Rickmansworth. We took only 21½ mins. for this 17.2 miles, and then came the long grind up to Amersham. Speed fell gradually till we were sustaining 31 mph up to the last mile – 850 drawbar horsepower, a fine effort at this relatively low speed; and after passing Amersham (23.6 miles) we just went like the wind.

It was no brief spurt; the effort was sustained at top pressure for a full 50 miles, and it was only when we were north of Rugby and getting several minutes ahead of time that Driver France eased his engine, ever so slightly. Through the beautiful

120

The inaugural GCR train about to leave Marylebone station on the 9th March 1899. Fred France had by now risen to fireman and is on the left of the cab, whilst at the controls is Harry Pollitt, the designer of the loco, no.861 a 4-4-0 class 11A. To the right is a silver lever, by which the Minister, Col. Ritchie will 'start' the train. (LLRRO, *Newton Coll.*)

In 1906 a more heavily loaded 'Sheffield Special' is climbing the Chilterns near Chorley Wood with vigour. It is hauled by a new class 8D Atlantic no.258, named 'The Rt Hon. Viscount Cross GCB, GCSI'. Designed by Robinson to explore the use of compounding, it showed only a marginal improvement in coal consumption. *(John Gercken Coll.)*

woodland scenery of the Chilterns we raced; 74 mph before Great Missenden; 55½ over Dutchlands and 82 near Stoke Mandeville, prior to a slight easing up before Aylesbury. Grendon Underwood Junction, 44.8 miles by this route, was passed in 53¾ mins and the long stretches of the 1 in 176 ascent north of Calvert were taken with no lower speed than 55¾ mph. *Jutland* passed through Woodford at full speed in 74¾ mins from Marylebone (69.2 miles). At Charwelton water troughs the speed was 64 mph, and 84 mph down Staverton Road bank; Rugby "hump" was cleared at 65½ and the speed rose again to 73 mph on the descent over the LMS viaduct. It was at this point that Driver France began to ease up a little; the lowest speed of his engine on the Lutterworth bank was 54 mph. Then came the final descent to Leicester Central Station, where *Jutland* was taken quite easily for the Great Central, not exceeding 76¼ mph; with a finishing time of 104¾ mins for the 103.1 miles from Marylebone."

Richard Hardy, who came to know Fred France well after his first journey with him on the 4.55pm to Leicester on the footplate of no.5506 class 11F (an 'improved' Director named 'Butler- Henderson'), comments that "Fred was a hard runner but not a heavy driver. Like all Neasden men he took liberties with the 25mph speed restriction through Rickmansworth. The speeds at Chorley Wood and the time taken for the 2.2 miles were always revealing. 40mph was normal and then the engine was set so that it gradually lost speed up the bank - thus saving coal water and the fireman's back - passing Amersham on time or nicely ahead. No speedometers then of course. He had an excellent reputation and 'had done it all' by the time he retired, in 1937."

Driver Fred France - easily recognised by his distinctive profile - now based at Neasden LNER and nearing the end of his distinguished railway career. Here he is pictured at Amersham station in 1936 and, as usual, at the controls of no.5506, an ex-Robinson 4-4-0 class 11F (LNER D11), 'improved' Director 'Butler-Henderson'.   *(R H N Hardy)*

Stationmen - Bob Clarke & Bob Butcher

The two well-known stationmen at Amersham, in the twilight of their careers on the Joint, with a combined service of 100 years. *(R N H Hardy)*

Right: Bob Clarke was recruited by the LNER to work on the Joint in 1935. He started at Chesham as a parcel boy on just £1 per week and subsequently worked at most of their stations. He recalls many incidents during the last war and the annual visit of Bertram Mills Circus by special train to Chalfont & Latimer for their winter quarters.

Left: Bob Butcher started work at Quainton Road station, having a lot to do with the relaxed workings of the Brill branch. Here he witnessed the notorious occasion when a loose-shunted wagon ran onto the mainline and hit a passing engine. Like all Joint staff he could be asked to act as a relief on any part of the Met - or GCR systems!

BACK TO THE FUTURE

In my last book I ended with a review of the likely evolution of the Joint and the impact on it of other likely railway developments. Sadly, subsequent events have thrown most of these expectations into the melting pot and, following what seemed to be a period of re-birth of railways in the UK, their future is again very unsettled.

To re-cap, the existing Conservative legislation to privatise British Railways was, somewhat surprisingly, implemented by the incoming 1997 Labour government with its Integrated Transport White Paper in 1998. A key feature of this was the addition of an overarching Strategic Rail Authority, above the existing Office of the Rail Regulator, to oversee the activities of Railtrack (the infrastructure provider), the franchised train operating companies (TOC's) and the multitude of sub-contractors.

However, since then the position of the UK railways has changed dramatically. Initially the impact of increasing demand had led to growth in the use of railways for both passenger (26%) and freight (34%) traffic, leading to recognition of the positive role that they could play in reducing road traffic. But more recently this perception of the resurgence of the railways has been thrown into doubt as a result of deteriorating performance attributed to basic faults in the method of the privatisation, centering on the effect of fragmentation of the industry. Users saw a lack of integration of services giving rise to increasing complexity and declining performance. As far as the TOC's are concerned, the whole operation of the franchising process has created delays and uncertainty, whilst adding bureaucracy to the inevitable hiatus in re-starting a dormant rolling stock industry to supply the desperately needed new trains.

Similar problems of lack of clarity and responsibility appeared to be at the heart of the troubles of Railtrack. The original concept of a lean organisation operating an internal market and contracting-out most of its activities on a competitive basis (to companies who often pass these on to yet further sub-contractors), had in practice shown weaknesses in management, co-ordination, planning, implementation, financial control, and the loss of traditional engineering skills. The lack of clear responsibilities which compromised reliability and safety culminated in a series of major disasters including Clapham, Watford, Southall, Paddington, Hatfield and Potters Bar, which demonstrated that the existing track and signalling infrastructure was in a state of disrepair due to under-investment.

The financial consequences of the inability of Railtrack to sustain the existing network, together with the escalating costs of their delayed major upgrade projects (such as the WCML), led in October 2001 to the Transport Minister, Stephen Byers, putting Railtrack into administration. Amid much controversy, he indicated that he would seek to reform the company on a 'not for profit' Public-Private-Partnership basis and at the same time, the regulatory regime would be 'streamlined'. Immediately Sir Alistair Morton (SRA) resigned and the Tom Winsor (ORR) post is expected to be absorbed into a new SRA under Tom Bowker. Nevertheless, the SRA had earlier been tasked with creating the strategy for railways in the UK and therefore its views on the future structure of the Joint and adjacent lines are of interest. The first SRA study was issued as 'A Strategic Agenda' in February 2001, giving a 'Wish List' for the desirable development of railways in the UK. Of particular relevance to the old Joint line were their plans for the projects to the north west of London as follows:

Chiltern Railways: After open competition, the existing franchise of M40 Trains was renewed for 20 years from 2003 and the main elements of their tender have been endorsed by the SRA. Firstly, the Marylebone - Birmingham route (partly the old GW & GC Joint Cttee. Line) to be considerably upgraded by 2003 with 1) two new platforms at Marylebone and the re-furbishing of Birmingham Moor St. station, giving an extra 50% capacity and up to 15 trains/hour; 2) completion of restoring the double track; 3) a new station at Warwick Parkway - now open - and upgrading of others; 4) extension to Stourbridge in 2001 and Kidderminster in 2002; 5) introduction of more Clubman type 168 'Turbostar' diesels; 6) an additional stock depot at Wembley; and 7) continued application of their proven automatic train protection system to all stock.

Secondly, a parallel improvement of the Aylesbury line was approved with train frequency increased by 75% and an upgrade of the type 168 'Turbostar' multiple diesel trains, some of which will undertake the journey in 40 minutes. The tracks are to be upgraded, including the LUL section, with the growth of passengers using Chiltern Railways at the expense of the Met likely to continue. Interestingly, in the context of the old Joint line, M40 Trains will remodel Aylesbury station and are encouraged to re-open the line beyond Aylesbury via a new Parkway station at North Aylesbury and on to Winslow (for Buckingham, Milton Keynes and the M1). Thus not only is part of Watkin's Met & GC route to be brought back to life, but other concepts of his are again to be considered, including an interchange station at West Hampstead with the Met and also a link to Oxford, which rekindles one of Watkin's early proposals for the Oxford & Aylesbury Tramway! Even the potential for re-opening part of the ex-Great Central mainline is to be examined.

East-West Link: The SRA also supported re-examination of the 1999 proposal to re-open the old LMSR line from Bedford and Sandy via Bletchley, Verney and Claydon Junctions - with connections to Aylesbury as above, Bicester and Oxford. This would give a cross-country route of increased clearance for container traffic and, avoiding London, between the west via Oxford and the eastern towns of Cambridge, Ipswich, Norwich and to the east coast ports. Some of this work at Claydon was included in the SRA's plans for the enhancement of the Chiltern Line and, whilst there has been some building on the old track bed in the Bedford area, the SRA regarded this project as feasible and of medium scope.

North-South Freight Route: A possible new freight railway was proposed by a private company, Central Railway plc, some ten years ago in order to 'provide increased capacity for freight trains between the Channel Tunnel, London and the North through the provision of a dedicated new line, partly formed from the former Great Central route'. With some support from midland and northern industry, but intense opposition from householders in the south who believe that their properties would be de-valued, the project appears to be in limbo. Government seem unwilling to support the necessary enabling legislation, much to frustration of Central Railway, who gave an 'ultimatum' to the Minister, John Prescott, in 2001 to the effect that they would withdraw if not backed by the Government. Getting no response, the backers of the Central Railway are now trying to encourage a 'private members bill' in order to progress matters. The SRA strategy merely noted that the proposal is being studied as a possible option within a window of over ten years. In practice any use by Central Railways of the infrastructure currently used by Chiltern Railways would give the latter the right to re-negotiate their franchise.

CrossRail: Also in 2001 the SRA reported favourably to the Government on this proposal, originally launched by London Transport in 1965, which was based on a new deep-level 6m diameter tunnel under London from Paddington to Liverpool Street to provide relief to the tube network. Connections would be made to Shenfield in the east and Neasden and Heathrow in the west. CrossRail trains would run from Aylesbury replacing existing Met trains, before joining the new line from Neasden, whilst the Met services from Watford and Uxbridge would continue to use the existing route to Baker Street. For CrossRail services west of London the present station platforms would need to be considerably lengthened and the route clearances adapted for overhead electrification.

Although much preparatory work was undertaken by LT, by 1996 interest faltered due to the escalating cost and the uncertainty over the future role of LT, to the extent that the project relapsed to a small team 'safeguarding the route'. Since then there have been many studies by such bodies as The City of London, Ove

Arup and Imperial College - all with positive support. Indeed, there is general recognition of the need to implement CrossRail but the problem seems to be the difficulty in making the decision on how it should be funded. However, in the run-up to the 2001 General Election, the Government announced that it was giving £154million for the development of the detailed plans by a Cross London Rail Ltd for the £3.8billion main tunnel under London. This initiated fresh debates and delay as to whether, as a second phase of the development, branches should be built to Heathrow in the west and Docklands in the east. However, in any event before any construction starts, the future of LUL and the role of the Mayor of London and his Transport for London (TFL) body has to be fully resolved.

The SRA remit appears to exclude the London Underground Ltd. system and thus there was no mention of the **Metropolitan Line.** Although there is general agreement that the LUL infrastructure is in urgent need of repair and upgrading which requires massive new investment, the lack of any agreement on how to proceed is severely delaying any practical action. In 1997 the incoming Labour Government made it clear that they wanted to achieve this investment by means of Public-Private-Partnership schemes in which private companies would bid to take over responsibility for the infrastructure (track, maintenance, signalling, stations and buying new trains) with the relevant parts of London Underground Ltd. operating the trains. By 2001 LUL had established "shadow Ops Co's" for the envisaged bid routes i.e.(1)sub-surface Metropolitan & Inner Circle and deep tube lines; (2)Bakerloo, Central & Victoria; and (3)Jubilee, Northern & Piccadilly. However the actual bidding process became chaotic. Firstly, it had been expected that Railtrack would have been a major contender but after the string of mainline disasters on their system, the Government felt that they were not sufficiently competent to participate in the London Underground contracts. Secondly, the Government-inspired devolution scheme for Greater London surprisingly resulted in the election of a Labour Party maverick, Ken Livingstone, as the new London Mayor. He held strong views that the PPP approach was expensive and, by fragmenting responsibility, repeated the mistakes of the earlier privatisation of BR. Instead, he wanted to use a bond issue to raise the capital for the necessary investment for modernisation. To emphasise his case for centralised responsibility he has created a body 'Transport for London' headed by Bob Kiley (a former head of New York Transportation) and in 2001, took the disagreement over the form of financing and safety issues to Court, whilst the Government tried desperately to complete the bidding the PPP process in order to create a *fait accompli.*

Whilst court actions continued the preferred bidders for the four LUL systems were chosen in 2002: Tubelines (Amey, Jarvis & Bechtel) for the Jubilee, Northern & Piccadilly lines; Metronet (Balfour Beatty, W S Atkins, Adtranz, Seeboard & Thames Water) for the Bakerloo, Central & Victoria Lines; Metronet for the Metropolitan & Circle lines. By July 2002 the litigation of Livingstone & Kiley had cost some £4M and as a result they withdrew their blocking action leaving the Government free to pursue their PPP approach to modernise LUL. However, Kiley still seeks a commitment to Government funding for CrossRail before he initiates the necessary enabling legislation.

Equally there was no mention by the SRA in their 'wish list' of the long-envisaged **Croxley - Watford** rail link, which would complete the useful missing link between the Watford branch of the Joint and the close-by ex-BR Croxley Green station and thereby enable trains to transfer between the Joint and the WCML. It would be a short link, but involves a major rail flyover above the roundabout near the ex-BR Croxley station. The estimated cost in 2000 was some £48m. Various local government, LUL and Railtrack consortia have failed to raise the necessary funds and although Transport for London regard it favourably, Hertfordshire County Council. - being the lead body - describe it as 'being on the back-burner'. However, later in 2001 the SRA stated that it was to proceed with the plans to re-instate rail services over the 2.75 mile route between Watford Junction and Croxley Green. A new station is to be built at Ascot Road and the mothballed Watford West station is to be refurbished. This gives some encouragement, as the work forms part of the envisaged link.

As this book is written the Future of the Joint seems clouded by the latest uncertainty that now afflicts much of the development of the UK rail network. Following the uproar at the end of 2001 over the decline in the state of railways in the UK and the loss of viability of Railtrack, the SRA was re-vamped under a new Chairman (Richard Bowker - ex-Virgin Railways). He quickly issued a SRA 'Strategic Plan' in January 2002, likening it to a 'Shopping List', demonstrating commitment, as compared with the earlier 'Wish List'. However, in reality it appeared to be a 'slimmed down' version of the earlier document, containing less detail about specific developments. Indeed the only commitments pertinent to the area of the Joint confirm the plans for Chiltern Railways and support for the Bedford-Bletchley link. There is virtually no mention of any of the other earlier relevant proposals! However the SRA also indicate that they wish to reduce the number of TOC's so that each of the London termini is only served by one company in order to reduce conflicting operations. Obviously this would reinforce the position of Chiltern Railways at Marylebone.

Thus at this point it also seems likely that the Central Railway proposal will fail and Chiltern Railways will be able to implement their plans to enhance and extend northwards over the old Joint line. The prospects of the other partner in the old Joint, the Met, depend on political wrangling and obtaining new trains to replace the over 40 year old A stock (which are currently showing severe signs of fatigue

APPENDIX 3: MISCELLANY

Top left:- Early picture of the post near Great Missenden marking the division between Met and GCR maintenance responsibilities. **Top right**:- Joint signs at Harrow station in 1939. **Centre**:- Met & LNER Joint uniform button *(Clement Cargill)*. **Bottom left**:- MetroLand carriage handle. **Bottom right**:- Pre-Joint Agreement excursion advert of about 1900.

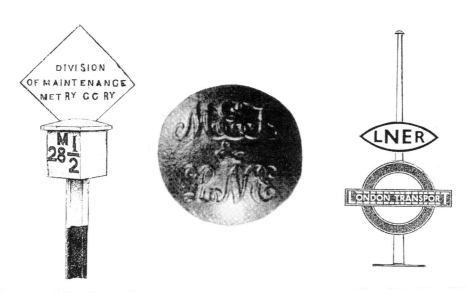

Metropolitan and Great Central Railways.

BUCKINGHAM MARKET.

MARKET TICKETS, THIRD CLASS,
ARE NOW ISSUED ON

SATURDAYS

FROM

AYLESBURY TO **BUCKINGHAM**

Return **1/11** Fare,

AVAILABLE ONLY BY FOLLOWING TRAINS:—

		A.M.	A.M.	A.M.
AYLESBURY	...dep.	7 30	9 47	11 45
BUCKINGHAM	... arr.	8 52	11 4	P.M. 2 12

RETURNING ON DAY OF ISSUE ONLY.

		P.M.		P.M.
BUCKINGHAM	...dep.	3 8		5 43
AYLESBURY	... arr.	4 2		6 37

APENDIX 4: APOCRYPHA

"In 1928 a young boy called Gordon was offered a birthday treat by his aunt. She suggested Bertram Mills Circus followed by a high tea at a Lyons Corner House. However Gordon, being an ardent railway enthusiast, pleaded for a trip through MetroLand from Liverpool Street to Verney Junction in a Met Pullman train. He was somewhat surprised when she readily agreed and they both thoroughly enjoyed the outing. Years later he found out that she had agreed to the venture because it was an opportunity to sip a plentiful supply of gin and tonics en route."

"A clerk at the LT headquarters was given the task of clearing the Chairman's office due to a new appointment. There he found the last independent Met timetable and in it someone had written 'watch Selbie, he is a slippery customer'. On referring it to his boss, he was told to burn it".

"During the construction of the main over-bridge at Neasden in 1937-8, a forge man had been tossing red hot rivets to the riveter. Unfortunately when the fire in the forge suddenly flared up watchful passers-by hastily called the fire brigade. When they arrived it seemed to be a rather trivial incident and, on connecting the hoses, took aim - missed the fire - and scored a direct hit on the positive rail! The electric current took the easiest route back to earth via the firemen who either jumped or were transfixed - just before the main circuit breaker came out at Wembley Park".

"After the last war, an early-morning fast City train of Dreadnought coaches left Chesham in torrential rain. By the time it reached Rickmansworth, for the change over to electric haulage, the luggage racks were full of passengers' wet coats, hats and umbrellas. The next stop was at Moor Park (for Sandy Lodge) and another sodden passenger squeezed in and added his raincoat to the rest on the rack. As usual the powerful Bo-Bo electric loco accelerated rapidly - tipping the soaking clothes on to a bowler-hatted city gent- who boiling with anger, said to the culprit - 'this is a Meropolitan line train - not a ****** wardrobe!'. "

"When he was a boy, Christopher lived with his family near to North Harrow station. On Sundays they often used go for a picnic on the picturesque Chorleywood common and, to his delight, watch the variety of trains on the Joint. One such day, they went to North Harrow in order to catch an Aylesbury train of Dreadnought coaches hauled by a Bo-Bo electric loco. However, when they opened the compartment door they were met with the sight of a sea of faces of children on an outing. Seeing there was little room, Christopher's father immediately picked him up and put him on the luggage rack!"

SOURCES

As this book is to an extent complementary to 'The Story of the MET & GC Joint Line', references shown below are *additional* to those quoted in the earlier book.

PRIMARY

MET 10/708	Allocation of responsibilities for the Joint	
	London Metropolitan Archive Acc.1297	1931
P/UC 158	Plans for Met. Rly. Quainton Road - Moreton Pinkney Extension	
	Bucks Record Office	1890
N.H.Green	Proposed Extension to Moreton Pinkney from Quainton Rd.	
	Deposited Papers. Bucks Record Office	1986
912.42151	MS&LR Extension to London. Line no.12-Sheet 8/65	
	Westminster City Archive Centre. Acc. III IU/5	1892
F Palmer	Plans of Land held by the 'Joint' in Chesham Vale	
	1) 'Joint' Correspondence	1931
	2) LT Correspondence	1981

SECONDARY

Christian Barman	The Man Who Built London Transport *(Pick)*	
	David & Charles	1979
Desmond Croome	The Metropolitan Chesham Branch	
	Underground News no.484 p167	2002
David Hodgkins	The Second Railway King *(Watkin)*	
	Merton Priory Press	2002
Michael J Smith	Metropolitan Freight	
	Back Track Vol.15 No.9 p510 and No.10 p599	2001
James R Snowdon	Metropolitan Railway Rolling Stock	
	Wild Swan Publications	2002
P Stears	BR Steam Operating No.3 (M'bone - Rugby)	
	Xpress Publishing	2001
Michael Turner	Handbook of MET & GC Jt. Cttee. Luggage Labels	
	RPS-H111 Railway Print Society	2001
SRA	A Strategic Agenda	2001
SRA	The Strategic Plan	2002

oooooO000ooooo

REAR COLOUR ILLUSTRATIONS

Page 137 Top: During the last war, the Met Bo-Bo electric locomotives were given a plain grey livery and had their nameplates removed as an economy measure. Some remained like this for a number of years and here, at Harrow on the Hill in 1954, is no.3 (ex- 'Sir Ralph Verney') waiting with a rake of Dreadnought coaches in platform no.1. *(Colour-Rail LT267/R O Oakley)*

Page 137 Bottom: Following the completion of the post-war electrification to Chesham in 1960, the delivery of the new aluminium A60 multiple electric stock was late. This illustrates the interim period when a 3-car set of old Met T stock operated the Chesham 'Shuttle'. Soon the parcel trolley and goods sidings were to become redundant. *(Colour-Rail LT276/R Oakley)*

Page 138 Top: In 1959, amidst a swirl of smoke, a 4MT 2-6-4T no.80140 running bunker-first, swings across into Aylesbury's up bay with Dreadnought stock to journey's end. This junction was re-laid as a result of the disastrous accident in 1904, which led to the formation of the Joint. *(Colour-Rail BRE1674/R Oakley)*

Page 138 Bottom: Winter 1963, with snow on the Chilterns at Little Missenden, as ex-LMS 4-6-0 Royal Scot class no.46111 'Royal Fusilier' climbs towards the summit with the 12.38 Marylebone - Nottingham Victoria train. *(Colour-Rail BRM 1258/J H Moss)*

Rear Inside Cover Top: Refurbished and freshly-painted for the Met Centenary train trip on the 26th May 1963, Bo-Bo electric locomotive no.5 'John Hampden' with matching Dreadnought coaches, waits in platform 3 at Baker Street station. *(Chris Miles)*

Rear Inside Cover Bottom: By the 1970's, the few remaining goods trains were hauled by diesel locomotives. One regular working was a refuse train from London to a large landfill site at Calvert, here seen passing through Aylesbury station, hauled by a class 25. *(Ron Potter)*

Rear Cover Top: A Gresley class V2 2-6-2 rolls through Amersham station with an up express from Sheffield in 1959. The new footbridge - yet to be painted - has just been erected to accommodate the new track layout for the LT electrification scheme. *(Colour-Rail BRE 1282/G H Hunt)*

Rear Cover Bottom: The core of the CrossRail project is a deep-level tunnel under London from Liverpool Street to Paddington. It is expected to extend this to Shenfield, Heathrow and also Aylesbury (where it would replace some Met/LUL services). This shows a mock-up of the proposed type 341 multiple electric units intended for the line. *(CrossRail)*